Road to N'Dondol

Heat, Sand, and Friends

by Allen W. Fletcher

All text and photos by Allen W. Fletcher
Cover photo: *Gana Sene*
ISBN: 978-0-615-28598-6

Published by Worcester Publishing Ltd.
101 Water Street, Worcester, MA 01604
Copyright © 2009 by Allen W. Fletcher
All rights reserved
Printed in the United States of America

Designed by Linda Dagnello

Preface

From 1969–71, courtesy of the remarkable institution called the Peace Corps, my wife Nina and I lived in the Senegalese village of N'Dondol, about 100 miles inland and about ten miles off the main road that extends east from Dakar all the way into Mali. The country—the historical territory of a number of different tribal empires—had been colonized by the French and heavily influenced by Islam.

A sparsely forested grassland typically described as savannah, our area was the traditional domain of the Serrer, who were sedentary farmers and herders. The core population of the village was Wolof, with the surrounding compounds and outlying villages being Serrer. In general, the Wolof were regarded as more citified—more deeply involved in a money economy and more strongly Islamic in their beliefs—while the Serrer were regarded as country folk—closer to their agricultural and animist traditions. Our closest friends were Serrer.

Over the course of two years, these people put up with us and took care of us, allowing us to participate as fully as two young *toubabs* could in the daily rhythms and yearly cycles of their lives. We attempted a few projects—literacy, latrines—and coped with the mundane discomforts of heat, illness and boredom. Mostly, however, we simply lived there, absorbing the richness of their way of life and providing them with a frequent source of amusement and interest.

We came to believe that the village life and rural splendor of the Serrer were in the process of being eroded inexorably by factors outside of their control—drought, demographic patterns, formal education, economic development, politics—and that the wholeness and simplicity of their lives were being lost to the double-edged machinery of modernity.

I wrote these stories in the early '70s. Everything in them is true, although sometimes condensed in time and undoubtedly romanticized. In editing them, I have been unable to fully excise a kind of didacticism running through them—a bending-over-backwards compulsion to explain things. There was simply so much I wanted to convey, and I didn't think that I had enough pure narrative to carry it all. As it is, there were memories left on the cutting room floor that it pained me not to include. So be it.

And I apologize for the Wolof. When I originally wrote these stories I had the idea that if a reader actually pronounced a little bit of Wolof it would have a sort of magical power to connect them to what I was writing about. I still feel that way, but I realize it's essentially an indulgence—a symptom of my own distress at feeling memory evaporate. So I left most of it in, and I also left it written—more or less—in French phonetics. I did loosen up somewhat on the translation, however, to pull it away from the formality that literal translation tends to imply. These people were farmers, after all—*beykats*, not *vrais sauvages*.

I visited the village in the mid-'80s; Nina 20 years after that. I think it is safe to say that life there has gone on quite effectively without us. The waters of their lives closed very quickly around whatever disturbance we made in them; the ripples continue to spread in our own.

Contents

Introduction viii

Chapter 1: Djinn 1

Chapter 2: Beying 9

Chapter 3: Réunion 23

Photographs 63

Chapter 4: Laobé 77

Chapter 5: Adjuma 97

Chapter 6: Boré 109

Chapter 7: Coq 139

Introduction

Baddu Sene and Bity Sene

I have in my mind a particular moment towards the end of our two years in the village.

Bity and I had just finished filling our *baignoirs* at the well behind the Diouf compounds and were about to carry them back to give to our horses. The weight of the tub of water pressed down on my head, straight through my neck, my spine, my hips, my legs, my heels, down into the African sand. The tub tipped slightly, and the water shifted its mass with a treacherous slosh; but I reacted subliminally, adjusting my balance skillfully enough to cushion its surge without overcompensating. No water had spilled. No spasm of panic had amplified the shifting of the load. I had not even glanced upwards to verify what was happening atop my head.

I looked around me: There was the well, and Bity coiling the rope, and the grass roofs of the Diouf compounds; and there was Aliou Diouf passing by on a path up the way, against a sandy panorama of cleared fields and thorn trees. And suddenly, soundlessly, everything seemed to pause for a moment in the shimmering white African heat. I stared at the scene: This was Africa before me. It looked just like the Africa I had always dreamed of; and yet it was utterly different. And the difference had just taken me by surprise. The Africa of the picture book had become the Africa of everyday life, and in the process had become something totally other than I had ever imagined it might be.

The difference, of course, was one of meaning. Every detail of the picture now had real meaning for me. I had watched Bity's father make that water bag. I had watched Tchekumba Sene make that rope. And that man passing by was not some noble savage on the African savannah — it was my friend Aliou Diouf, walking a path that I knew well to a grove of trees that I saw every day, hunched a little bit with embarrassment because he knew that we knew that he was late — that he was supposed to go out there on Thursday to wash himself with a particular magic charm, and here it was Friday. The difference resided in every aspect of the scene around me, as I stood there accommodating the subtle shiftings of the washtub of water, feeling its weight press my heels into the sand in the midday heat.

There are moments in coming to know another place and another people and another way of living when the strangeness ceases to be strange and one feels the shock of the familiar. Standing in the sand watching Aliou Diouf pass by I could feel for a moment in what ways it was exactly the same as standing on the lawn at home in Worcester, Massachusetts, watching a neighbor pass by; and in what ways it was totally different. And in the moment when the two were superimposed, and my mind floated in a short tunnel between this home in Senegal and that one in Massachusetts, I was able to understand more fully than ever before what it meant to be a human being on the Earth.

Since this glimmer of understanding was unique in my life, and since none of the marvelous technology which has brought about the shrinking of the world seems able to duplicate it, I have not yet stopped trying to convey to others what persists in being meaningful about it to me. It should go without saying that this sort of insight is not unique in the world; but it still seems far too unique to be left unsaid.

And so I have made this little book to try to convey a feeling of what it meant to live with some particular people in a particular village in a particular place on the earth at a particular time in their own history. It has been an elusive and rewarding task.

Memory is a capricious faculty. I can sit and consciously reconstruct a scene in my mind with greater and greater completeness without having it truly transport me; and I can be walking along the street thinking of nothing at all and catch a smell which jolts me instantly back to the village. Such is the integrative power of the sense of smell, which can convey in an instant what all the mind's labor cannot accomplish.

I think it is just possible that if you look at these pictures and read these stories and then try to hold them in your mind at once — look into old Gana's eyes and remember who he is, and think of Adjuma shuffling off on his fool's errands — that you will catch a whiff of Africa. And in the moment before that scent disappears you may understand who you are just a little bit better. And if this happens, it will have been worth it for both of us.

— Berkeley, 1974

Chapter 1

Djinn

Djinn

It must have been midnight. The universe outside our mosquito netting appeared to be in order. A few familiar night sounds filtered in: The horse outside the window tore a mouthful of straw from the thatch of his hut and munched on it quietly; a lizard scurried across the wall out in the breezeway; one of the never-seen creatures who lived up in the rafter space skittered across the ceiling. Beyond our net cocoon, beyond our cement block walls, beyond our millet stalk fence, the village and surrounding countryside were resting, respiring evenly, gathering themselves for another onslaught by the African sun.

Peace reigned and the earth had cooled. So why was I wide awake and sweating? Nini was awake too. We held our breath and strained our ears for something which might be eluding us. Nothing. We looked at each other in the near-darkness, puzzled. I propped myself up on one elbow and felt a bead of sweat trickle slowly down my side to the sheet. We waited. Nothing.

I slid outside the netting and carefully, soundlessly, pulled on my pants. There was half a moon out, and I wouldn't need the flashlight. I grasped it anyway and crouched by the netting in silence. Nothing. Nothing.

Suddenly the stillness erupted in cacophony as both horses pierced the night with cries of alarm, joined instantaneously by horses over in the Sene and Diouf compounds. Their shrillness clutched at my heart and cast a web of dissonance across the village.

As I started out the back door they ceased their clamor, but the rooster immediately took over with a series of raucous crows. It was quite light by the moon, and I could see nothing unusual. Bill, the horse we kept behind the house, paced nervously. The rooster continued his alarm, and his hens fussed in the shadows. I stepped out onto the fine, cool sand and walked around to the front. Joe was also upset under his ragged roof. He danced back and forth between two holes which he had long ago eaten in the fence and which commanded views of the surrounding fields. I felt the thud of his hooves in the sand and watched his grey flank moving in the shadows. Nothing seemed out of place. Behind the house the rooster screamed one more time and fell quiet.

I went to the gate and looked across to the silent compounds before me and the fields and trees stretching away off to the left. The soft night air embalmed me, and the stars vibrated overhead in crystal cold silence. Had it passed? A sudden shrieking startled me, and a flock of birds swarmed into the sky from a cluster of trees beyond the nearby fields at whose feet lay a group of graves. Their shrill cries continued as they flew overhead, turned, and retreated. I strained to see if they were birds or bats, but they were gone too soon, funneling back into the trees and leaving the night to itself once more.

It was over. The earth continued its silent exhalation up to the stars. Joe munched on some straw back inside the fence. The fields, cleared for the approaching rainy season, glowed pale in the moonlight before me. Had anything happened at all?

Someone was approaching from under the trees by the Sene compounds, whistling as he emerged into the moonlight. It was Bity. I felt relieved that someone else had been disturbed—someone who had known this sand, these trees, these stars, this night for a lifetime. We greeted each other in customary fashion, with a tacit touch of humor at the routine, as if to affirm that unseen presences would have to do a lot more than this to disturb the normal affairs of men.

"*Mba djam ngam* [I hope you have peace]."

"*Djam a-rek* [Peace only]."

"*Mba yip chi keur-gi ngi chi djam* [I hope everyone in the house is in peace]."

"*Djam a-rek, kai* [peace only]."

"*Fall* [my name]."

"*Sene* [his name]."

"*Fall*." We shook hands.

This was the third night that this had happened. Bity had heard it the previous two nights; and he had come over tonight because he knew we were nervous. During our year and a half in the village he had become the equivalent of a wilderness guide for us, the wilderness being the space-time of his own village. He was sensitive to the many ways in which we misunderstood and misinterpreted his world. At times like this, when something about it had once again confounded us, he wore a smile which said, simply: "This is what our world is like. What you just felt may be frightening, but it is also ordinary. It is part of the world we live in."

We talked together at the gate and then saw to the animals. He said that the first night he had thought that a stray horse had passed by, but now he thought that it had probably been a *djinn*—that animals and especially horses were always the first to sense these things. He assured me that they never or rarely entered a compound. I asked if it had anything to do with the old *laobé*, Baddu's grandfather, whom we had buried over in one of those graves the previous week. He said that it was possible but that he thought it was just a djinn passing by, and he reminded me of some similar incidents that had occurred up near the Diouf compounds.

I knew about djinns well enough from countless stories which he and others had told us. There was really little left to say. Our talk passed on to other things—to the horses, to the approaching rainy season—and then we bade each other good night.

"*Fananalen* [May you sleep]…"

"*Ak djam* [with peace]."

"*Amin* [Amen]."

"*Yalla nenyu yeo ak djam* [May Allah let us wake in peace]."

"*Amin.*"

I watched from the gate as he crossed the open space to his own compound and disappeared into the shadows. Around me the cleared fields glowed softly in the moonlight, and the nearest trees stood etched against their background in poised silence. For a year and a half I had walked this sand, coaxed plants out of it, drawn water from it. And over that course of time I had spent so many evenings, so many hours sitting and listening to stories of *djinns* and *rabbs* and the like that I had simply stopped disbelieving in them. They were an inextricable part of this world which had been shown to us—a hue or texture which ran through every part of the life and landscape of the village and which became more distinct the more we participated in it.

The landscape of the village was utterly different now from when I had first encountered it. Everything about it was imbued with meaning, laid down by the accumulated experience of everyday life. It was more vivid and familiar and yet more intensely strange that I had ever imagined that it could be.

The land was flat, what I had always imagined to be described by the term savannah except that it was farmed quite intensively by the people who lived upon it. Divisions between fields which had been at first invisible to me were quite apparent now, following the implications of the terrain and the social history of the Serrer people. Here in front of me was Saliou Diouf's bean field; beyond it, old Gana's field of millet; beyond that my own. The general impression was one of cultivated grassland, whose particularities one only learned as one participated in it.

Cultivated and inhabited. The predominant feature upon the land was the trees, which grew in astounding and bizarre variety—seldom thick enough to be seen as a group and thus each with a presence of its own. The Wolof word for tree—*garab*—was also the general term for medicine and in particular what we call magic. Men who had knowledge [*kham-kham*] understood what garab to use to work particular effects. Other substances were employed as well, but clearly the most common ingredient in *garab* [medicine, magic] was *garab* [tree].

One never cut down a tree. Rabbs, the devils or spirits associated with each family, lived down in their roots; and djinns were known to hover near them at night. They were charged beings. The Serrer shared the land with them, farmed amidst them, lived in their shade and their protection.

The trees were not merely figures in the landscape; and they were not merely sources of plenty—whose leaves might be in the sauce for tonight's millet, whose nuts might be in the sauce next week, whose fruit one fed to one's goats, whose twigs one used to polish one's teeth, whose leaves one used to combat malaria, whose thorns one used to fence one's field, whose seeds one cast to tell the future, whose bark one stripped for rope, whose branches one used to make huts and tools and furniture, and whose shade one sought for relief from the scorching sun. They were charged beings, as well, and one knew them also as the habitats of spirits and embodiments of power, whose roots reached down to tap forces alive in the earth beneath one's feet and in whose embrace—never to be taken for granted—one established one's household.

Across the open space in front of my gate the millet stalk fences, grass roofs, and woven granaries of the Sene compounds merged with the shadows of the tree where Aliou Diouf had encountered a djinn one night which had clung to his back until he had dropped what he was carrying and run screaming down the path and into the nearest compound; Bity himself had seen lights in its branches one night. Beyond that was the well by the Diouf compounds to which Modou Diouf's father had fled one night from a djinn. He had dived down the well and traveled through the earth along the roots of trees, all the while pursued by the djinn, until he had been able to hide at a spot where two roots crossed. Finally, when it was safe, he had surfaced in N'Diamane two miles away.

Nearer than the well was the little grove of young baobabs, their bark stripped for rope, where Assane had strode back and forth in the moonlight on a night like this, ranting at the height of his rabb-bedeviled craziness about killing his brother and eluding the voices that were driving him mad. Nearer still was the odd-shaped root to which I had tied the stray horse which had come in the gate one night to fight with Joe; and the huge *bentenyi* which sheltered the ruined hut of the old leper who had played the *ridi* so beautifully; and the contorted *gigis* in whose branches lights had several times been seen at night. And over to the left past my field and old Gana's stood the trees by the graveyard from which the flock of birds had forayed into the night a half hour before.

The bare fields shimmered in silence. The stars shone down on a landscape which was simultaneously magical and mundane; and I could only wonder how it existed in the mind of someone who had been born into it. Did Bity experience what I did now, only more intensely; or was it, for him, something quite different? And Aliou, and Adjuma, and Saliou, Baddu, Latendeo, old Gana, Seidu?

Seidu had cautioned me earnestly the day before that if the animals sensed something again I was not even to look outside my house through the crack in the door. Well, perhaps a djinn had passed by and perhaps it hadn't, but we had survived; and I felt part of a whole in a way which I had never felt before. I was sleepy again. The air was cooler. I pissed in the sand beside the gate and returned to the house.

Later, at what must have been three or four in the morning, filtered through layers of mosquito netting and sleep, we could hear the rhythmic thump of wood on wood as women in the Sene and Diouf compounds commenced their pounding of the next evening's millet while the air was still cool. Two or three coordinated their pounding to create a complicated rhythm which played on the periphery of our consciousness as we drifted back to join the rest of the village in sleep.

Chapter 2

Beying

Beying

We could never get up early enough. Sweat broke out on my brow as I sipped my coffee, clinging to the fleeting moments before the heat of the day could accumulate. During the dry season it was possible to do a significant amount of work during the morning in relative comfort; but now, when the work in the fields was imperative, there was only the briefest margin of respite. Sitting on the porch I tried to savor it, to nurse it, to prolong the moment; but all I felt was transition, imminence, gathering heat. There wasn't time enough to even flirt with staying home any longer.

"*Nyu dem* [Shall we go]?" Bity offered, addressing that which had become undeniable.

"*Aitcha, nyu dem.*"

We picked up our *gops*—Bity, Modou N'Gom and I—and went out at the gate. Between us and Modou Yatte's compound the foot-high millet, wet with dew, sparkled in the early morning sun. We saw Baddu across the way, hopping on one foot because of a sore in his ankle. We waved, and Bity called to him,

"*Kai nyu dem tollba* [Come on, let's go to the field]."

"*Bull ma meré way, Bity; suma gom da mitti* [Don't make me angry—my sore hurts]," he yelled back, bristling under Bity's tacit accusation of laziness.

"*Kon, nongi dem,*" Bity called back, and we turned up the path to our left.

Flies rose from the young millet to greet us, swarming about us like our own personal atmosphere and then settling to rest on our backs. Today we were carrying them to Bouboul, an area about a mile to the north, towards M'Bomboye, where Bity tended a field of millet. The sand of the path was not yet hot. It yielded familiarly to my feet, cushioning the forward impetus of each step, down-grading a brisk walk to a trudge.

We passed between Saliou Diouf's bean field on the right, meticulously lined with a border of *cad* tree thorns, and my own small field of millet on the left. The fringe of *bisap* I had planted along the path had not received enough rain to coax it out of the ground. Likewise my corn, which I had proselytized to skeptical ears, had failed to appear. Only the millet *soona* had come up, the poorest of the three strains commonly planted but the most responsive to minimal moisture; and the gourd vines which Bity's mother had planted in particular spots of her own choosing along our fence; and the grass and weeds. Even my millet had failed in some places, and in others it had been decimated by wayward goats and donkeys.

The field now to our right was all weeds. Our friend Bamboule, who had returned from Dakar for the rainy season to help his father, had already abandoned it in disgust. Old Gana's field now to our left was cleared of grass and weeds, but had little millet either.

"*Dow yey guru?*" Bity asked with a grin, reaching into his shirt pocket.

"*Aha kai,*" I completed the familiar exchange. *Dow yey guru? Aha kai!* [You won't chew some kola nut? On the contrary!]

He produced the soft pinkish brown nut and pried it open along its natural plane of cleavage, exposing its creamy white inner flesh. He gave half to me and I dug my thumbnail in, snapping off a piece and putting the rest in my pocket. Bity did the same beside me. I bit into my portion tentatively, releasing a pre-taste of its bitterness, and then crunched it into a mash between my molars. We walked along in silence; and now, here it came, the familiar numbing sensation starting at the back of the tongue and spreading slowly throughout the mouth as the little mash of kola granules and saliva seemed to expand like yeast. I reached up and pushed back a couple of particles which had drifted out onto my slightly numb lower lip.

"*Guru niekh-ne dé* [Kola is delicious]!" I affirmed to Bity, and he agreed. The bitterness of the nut infused my being, and I could feel its sharp aftertaste beginning to gather at the entrance to my throat. The sun was getting hot behind us as we plodded along past anonymous fields. I felt good.

A *tok* [hornbill] passed overhead in its comical dipsy-doodle flight. It would work to gain altitude and then glide, only to be pulled earthward by its large bill and have to flap back up once more. Modou left the path and ran through some young peanut plants to try to discern where the bird was headed. He was plotting the capture of its babies. The area we were passing through called to mind a city park, because of the curiously formal spacing of the larger trees. Foraging goats had contributed to the effect by pruning the bottoms of the low leafy *dakar* trees in a severe horizontal edge. I was on the lookout for a particular pair of huge black birds which I had seen here twice before. Called *gerokindobine*, they were larger than vultures, with beaks a foot and a half long and striking red and white patches on their shoulders. Bity knew what I was looking for and pointed one out before I could spot it. Shiny black and ominous, it seemed to crouch rather than perch on the thorny branch of a cad tree. As we approached it swooped grandly down and away, joined from an upper branch by its mate. Distinct white patterns showed on the backs of their huge black wings. They landed on the ground a hundred meters away and continued their retreat with great, hulking hops.

Bity had told me once that they could kill small children, although when I pressed him he acknowledged that he had never heard of it happening. His father, he said, used to shoot them, until he had given up hunting altogether. I shuddered to think of old Gana aiming his ancient rifle, imperious in his robes but with one damaged eye which gazed glassily in odd directions.

The three of us continued on, and the sun climbed in the sky behind us. A beautiful bird with feathers of iridescent blue-green flew past us into the stubby branches of a baobab. The tree's absurdly bloated trunk thrust out of the ground at an unlikely angle. Its shabby fuzz of new leaves failed to hint at the time when its voluptuous fruit would hang in long, perfectly vertical plum bobs, contradicting the grotesquity of the rest of the tree.

Modou was babbling excitedly beside me about the prospect of going swimming towards the end of the rainy season at a place far away on the other side of the village—Loukouk—where a clay-bottomed depression would fill up with water if there was enough rain. Here we were begging for rain, and he was talking about going swimming. I told him that I didn't believe that that much water could exist in one place, and he stumbled over his words as he tried to describe the wonder of it.

Indefatigably happy, Modou was Bity's *djourbat* [child of his sister] and had recently come to live with him from his own village farther south on the way to M'Bah Faye. Used to speaking his native Serrer, he was not yet comfortable with the Wolof which was demanded in the more cosmopolitan milieu of the village and which he had to speak with me.

He was a great boon to Bity because he loved to work. He had tried the first level of the school system three different times but had been unable to progress in that realm. I had never heard him utter a word in French. He thrived, however, on the myriad physical tasks of village life.

He was strong and healthy and liked nothing better than to throw himself into hard work. The gravest of occasions could not suppress his cheerful white-toothed smile.

"Modou N'Gom," Bity laughed at him now, *"Munogulo dara chi oulof* [You can't yet do anything in Wolof]." Modou shrugged helplessly at that which he could not control and continued his happy spiel. The smile never left his face.

The possibility of total immersion in water seemed doubly incredible to me—first because of the quantity of that precious element which would be required and secondly because of its promise of physical escape, which was otherwise unheard of in this land and culture. We had been warned of such pools because of the danger of schistosomiasis, but later on in the rainy season the unrelieved pressure of heat and flies and sores on my skin would drive me to it, and I would accompany Modou and Baddu on an expedition to Loukouk.

In a few more minutes we reached the field at Bouboul, one of six which Bity was cultivating that year. It was not in very good shape. The small amount of rain we had received had been marginal for the millet he had planted but quite adequate for the grasses. I had a hard time distinguishing the millet from the weeds. Already sweating, we set to work.

The farming tool, called a *gop*, consisted of a long wooden handle made by the *laobés* from a straight root or branch, with a half-moon shaped blade fitted to the end made by the *teugs* from some piece of salvaged metal. One sharpened it by hammering it thin at the edge. When one held the end of the handle at waist height the blade sat flat on the ground six feet away. On the forward stroke one stepped forward, thrusting the gop out to arm's length from the body, sliding the blade under the sand to sever the roots of the grass and weeds. On the return stroke one would clear back the loose vegetation, leaving a swath of bare sand. Once one developed an eye for what was to be spared and a feel for the precise width of the blade it was easy to establish a satisfying rhythm. The sun beat down, and we worked hard.

When we had planted my own field, my friends had insisted that we do it in straight rows, even though we were not using a planting machine. They said that planting in rows was more proper and beautiful. I had noticed, however, that they didn't bother to apply such Cartesian rigor to their own fields. This millet had been sown randomly. I had discovered that with a gop it was easier to cultivate a field like this than one sown in rows because there was a casual pick-and-choose quality to the work rather than the relentless progression from plant to plant, row to row.

Pick a spot; forward, back. Pick a spot; forward, back. I felt well-oiled with sweat and a little bit dizzy from the heat. Forward, back; forward, oops. On the return stroke the back of my blade encountered an unsevered root, and the handle slipped out of my relaxed hand.

"*Gop dannu-ne* [there goes the gop]!" Bity exclaimed, and we took a break. He had explained previously that the gop knew when it was time to stop working. In olden times when a gop took a notion to slip from someone's hands then everyone in the field would go home. We weren't that fastidious about the custom, but we welcomed the opportunity to rest. We sat at the base of a *dakar* tree, lit cigarettes, and shared some guru. I burrowed my feet in the sand to keep the flies off the sores on my toes. Modou N'Gom continued working with cheerful exuberance.

I tried to get Bity to estimate whether or not the current crop of millet would last through the following dry season. He said what everyone knew too well: We needed more rain. Last year's crop had been poor, but it had been stretched thin and was only now beginning to run out. This year there had been an auspiciously early light rain and then a couple of downpours, after which everyone had planted. Then the heavens had turned stingy, and for three weeks now there had been no rain. Almost daily, clouds would build to the south and then pass the village by. Men and women would stand in their fields with the young millet turning yellow around them, watching the storm clouds rumble and move on.

Bity talked of a year like this when the second wave of rains had come too late. The millet had already died in the ground and it was too late to plant again. The dry season that year had been so bad that the only food left to eat in the village had been baobab fruit. People would walk all night to the Catholic mission in Bambey when there was rumored to be a shipment of welfare food. People died. When I questioned him with astonishment, Bity laughed a laugh which I had heard many times before —a laugh which expressed embarrassment at having to give my innocent eyes a glimpse of how difficult their lives could be. It was the laugh of a people who understood that they were at the mercy of life, in an often inhospitable land.

Even in a good year this was the hardest time—early *nowette*, the rainy season. There was lots of work to be done and little to eat, and a brutal, humid heat stewed the land and the people on it. While the land turned green, human skin broke out in open sores, and people took turns with bouts of malaria.

The day was blazing hot even in the shade. We got up to resume our work, and I was careful to rise slowly. "*Nadge-bi tange-ne* [The blaze of the sun is hot]," Bity commented, and I agreed. It was too hot to stand around doing nothing, and we both sought refuge in the rhythm of the gop. Forward, back; forward, back. The patches of sand cleared by my blade glared white before my eyes. The sun burned through the shirt on my back.

Nadge-bi tange-ne, nadge-bi tange-ne. The image of the old woman who had taught me that phrase floated into my mind. "*Nadge-bi tange-*

ne, nadge-bi tange-ne!" she had shrieked, laughing maniacally and watching me in my discomfort as I visited her compound. I had thought that she was out of her mind. Her face swam before me now and the sun assaulted my body as I scratched at the hot dry sand of her homeland with my gop. She had spoken the truth after all, and the phrase was one whose meaning I had come to understand quite well. *Nadge-bi tange-ne*, I said to the earth; *nadge-bi tange-ne*, the sand glared back. Forward, I slid my blade under the weeds; back, I pulled their bodies clear. Forward, back, forward, back—*nadge-bi tange-ne, nadge-bi tange-ne, nadge-bi tange-ne té!*

"*Ndokh mungi nyo* [Here comes some water]," Bity broke my trance, and I looked up to see his mother, Tchab Dieng, approaching us on the path with a gourd of water on her head. Skinny little Abdou Dieye padded along beside her.

"*Jerrigen jiff*" she called, thanking us for our labors. "*Ndokh mangi* [Here's some water]."

"*Wow kai!*" we all three exclaimed, leaving the field and leaning our gops against the tree.

"*Yenengi ligé chi alabi rek, di bey rek, di nyakh rek,*" she said in singsong praise of our industry, "*Lolou mo back!*" [You all are just working in the fields, and farming and sweating. That's what is good!].

We suffered her effusiveness and lit cigarettes while she exclaimed at how much work we had accomplished and how dry the millet was. Abdou mimicked the way I smoked my cigarette and scurried out of reach when I lunged at him. He observed me inscrutably from a safe distance.

Bity tasted the water. "*Mandali!*" he exclaimed to Tchab with a smile, "*Kain nga am frigo, Dieng* [Since when have you had a refrigerator, Dieng]?" He handed me the gourd and I hung my face over it, breathing in its cool sweetness. I took enough to wash out my mouth and let a little slip down my throat. Having come from Nopili, the main well of the village, it was slightly salty. The four village wells yielded the only potable water within a sizable area of land, forcing women from surrounding villages to walk up to two and three miles to our village for their water. Rainwater, if it ever came, would save them a journey to the well and would taste better to boot. I handed the gourd to Tchab, who was shaking her head sadly at the field.

"Adouna, pot u ndah le," she said, quoting the first part of a Wolof saying [Life is the cup to the water jug: You drink, and you pass it to the next].

I took out another piece of guru and munched it quietly while Tchab talked to Bity in Serrer. Modou and Abdou had caught a large beetle and and were poking it around in the sand. I practiced the elusive art of ignoring the flies on my arms and legs. We all talked about the prospects for rain for a while, and then I picked up the water gourd. It had been about five minutes: The aftertaste of the guru sat waiting at the top of my throat. I took a mouthful, held it for an instant, and swallowed. There it was, one of the most exquisite taste sensations I had ever experienced. The water slid cool down my throat, and the aftertaste rose back up from its wake—sharp, clear, delicious. I took another swallow and there it was again—smooth and cool, sharp and clear. Two more swallows and the elixir had faded. I passed the gourd to Bity and leaned back against the tree. "*Ndokh-mi sede-ne* [that is cool water]," I sighed, closing my eyes.

"*Ndokh-mi sede-ne*" echoed Bity in a kind of a chant, tapping a rhythm on his box of Boxeur matches: "*Nadge-bi tange-ne, guru-gi niekh-ne, ndokh-mi sede-ne lol.*"

The heat of the day had gathered to its full height, and we remained in retreat under the tree. The little sores on my toes throbbed slightly, but the flies had thinned. I kept one hand flopping lazily by my face to keep them from landing on it. Bity and I lit cigarettes and talked about his fields. Two of his fields of millet would be all right if they received rain; this one and another one would at least be worth harvesting; the peanuts would be poor in any event.

Tchab was up working before the rest of us, picking her way slowly towards the far border of the field, seemingly immune to the heat of the day. Now and then she stopped to tend to a plant patiently by hand, leaning straight-legged from the waist with timeworn grace. Modou rose and accompanied her with his gop, sweeping out great patches of grass with boyish exuberance.

Bity was pensive. He said his mother had just told him that certain people in the village were talking about working some of the old Serrer magic in order to make it rain. He said that his father's father had been able to make it rain, and that he believed it still could be done. There was a definite sequence of steps which might be taken, but taking them was an extremely serious matter. I expressed my skepticism, and he assured me that there was much that could be done. I believed that I saw a tension in his eyes and in his smile—a fear of having traditional magic and knowledge put to the test. I shared that fear.

We rose together and entered the direct blaze of the sun. Behind us under the dakar tree Abdou Dieye began to cry. He was lonely, and fended off our shouts of good cheer. Bity said that the only work we had to accomplish was to clear the area over by his mother. The soil evidently was poorer there, and there were large patches where even the weeds had fared badly. It took us about an hour of steady work, while the sun beat down and little Abdou cried by himself under the dakar tree.

Bity, Modou, and I walked home the way we had come, with Abdou racing ahead of us on his skinny little legs and waiting for us to catch up. Tchab went off to help a friend in another field. The path, unprotected by any foliage, was burning hot and seemed to impede our progress more than before. I winced to myself whenever my bare toes or heel remained in contact with the sand for too long. Many of the fields had people working in them now, and we called out encouragement as we passed: *"Jerrigen jiff! Jerrigen jiff, way!"*

Aliou Diouf was working like a man possessed, the veins standing out on his neck and his eyes popping wide. Tchiachi Sene was weeding his peanuts with a cultivator, walking slowly between the rows while his son led the donkey ahead of him. We stopped to chat with him. As he turned to face us I noticed some leaves sticking out from beneath his knitted ski cap onto his forehead and realized that he had malaria. Sweat was dripping down his face. He and Bity shook their heads in the field. He looked at me and noticed the sores on my feet.

"Ah Fall," he said sadly, "Senegal niekhuk de [Senegal is no good]." We talked with him briefly and then continued home as he and his son and their donkey resumed their slow progress across the field.

We passed a file of women carrying tubs of water back to M'Bomboye, two miles away.

"Jerrigen jiff," they said to us as we passed.

"Jerrigen jiff, yen it," we replied.

Heat waves shimmered up from the white sand ahead of us, and a few clouds were building far beyond the village to the south. We passed the spot where the Catholic priests from Bambey had once set up a special box to catch spirits; we passed a hollow cad tree where honey bees had made a nest; we passed another cad whose recently-fallen limb had been stripped of thorns and was beginning to be cut up by the laobés. We passed the Serrer graveyard, the well by the Diouf compound, old Gana's field, my own field, and finally we were back at my front gate. In the sand over by the empty school room two donkeys were taking a dust bath, and from the peanut cooperative shed came the occasional metallic squeak of a sifting bin. Otherwise all was still in the tingling white heat.

Baddu was sitting with Nini on the front porch and greeted us moodily as we came in the yard. I heard a faint rumble to the south and called attention to it. Modou smiled at me hopefully, Baddu made a gesture as if I should know better, and Bity just laughed his apologetic laugh as we leaned our gops against the fence.

"*Chakharn rek le* [It's just kidding around]," he said, shaking his head with a grin: "*Lolou mut-ul dara: chakharn rek le* [that doesn't amount to anything; it's just kidding around]."

Chapter 3

Réunion

Réunion

N'Djamé Sene's boutique cast an early morning shadow across the sand of the street, and in its protection stood a horse and *charrette* and several clusters of people. Outside of its boundaries the sand was already getting hot. Emanating from the other side of the Wolof portion of the village, a slow, steady rhythm of drums had also begun to assert its presence. It colored the buzz of conversation outside the boutique with a strain of anticipation, preparation.

The charrette was about to leave, generating the usual flurry of chatter and confusion. The driver had finally arranged three woman passengers on the plank seats with their possessions about them and was looking around for Biran N'Dour, his fourth passenger, whose baggage took up most of the rear portion of the bed. Biran had disappeared, however, as was his habit at moments like this. The driver searched in vain and dispatched two children to look for the man. One of the women, her head in the sun because of the height of the charrette, climbed down and stood in the shade with some friends. Old Gana stood by the side of the charrette giving some lengthy instructions to the woman on the rear seat. The driver accepted a cigarette from a friend and fell to talking, giving up thoughts of a quick departure.

Up on the stoop stood Abdou Dieye and another man, talking to Cadere Dia, pleading earnestly about something, verging on anger. Guedj Sene, who had just bought cigarettes inside and who loved a good argument, stood in the doorway looking for an opportunity to enter the discussion. His brother, young Gana—*chef de village*—had just disappeared to the rear of the shop with N'Djamé Sene himself, talking distractedly about some matter related to the scheduled events of the day.

I was talking to Amadou Badiane, who lived close by and had been taking his morning stroll. Except for him, everyone here was present for some reason having to do with the imminent departure of either the charrette or N'Djamé's truck for the main road and points beyond.

The village lay six miles south of the paved road and railroad which ran east from Dakar all the way into Mali. The charrette would stop at the road, leaving its passengers to take bush taxis or *car-rapides* east or west to their destinations; and its driver would probably not return until after the heat of the day had passed. The hour and a half herky-jerky charrette ride became an eternity if the midday sun were allowed to compound its intrinsic discomforts. N'Djamé's Peugot 403 truck, on the other hand, could negotiate the sandy track in fifteen minutes; and he would have completed his business in Bambey, where he was now headed, and be back to the village before noon in time for the big political *réunion*.

N'Djamé was the richest man in the area, a Serrer from M'Bomboye who had established his household here in the N'Dondol Oulof, the Wolof portion of the village. Every morning he and his *apprenti*, Cadere, would drive off to Bambey, or Dakar, or one of the regional markets to spend the day buying and selling. Since acquiring his truck he had been able to increase his wealth dramatically. He had recently added a large cement brick storeroom behind his boutique and had replaced his wives' individual thatch huts with a cement barracks of single rooms opening onto the heart of his compound behind the boutique.

N'Djamé was the only person in the village with a functioning motor vehicle, which enabled him to participate in a different level of trade from the two or three other boutique owners. This allowed him to accumulate wealth, but also forced him to maintain quite a prodigious pace of commercial activity while the others stayed home and minded their stores. His boutique had become one of the foci of daily congregations of men in the village, the others being young Gana's boutique and the peanut cooperative. The little crowd here today was not unusual, although the background drums and the tense pitch of the voices set it apart from the ordinary.

I had walked down to give Cadere the key to our post office box in Bambey so that he could bring back our mail, a favor which I had accepted when he offered it because of the magnitude of discomfort which it saved me, even though I did not like to be in his debt. As N'Djamé's *apprenti*, his charge was the negotiation and execution of everything involving passengers and merchandise—hustling, deal-making, enticing, stonewalling, loading and unloading baggage. He was the perfect *apprenti*—tough, cocky and fast-talking—and he loved exercising the power which N'Djamé's employ gave to him. Right now he was fending off Abdou Dieye, his elder and an important man in N'Dondol Oulof, who wanted him to take a message to an official in Bambey. Guedj, emerging from the interior, was supporting Abdou's argument; but Cadere stood firm.

Back in the depths of the boutique his *patron* was still talking with young Gana. The latter, who had been in a frenzy of preparation for a week, was asking him to deliver a last-minute communication to some official and bring back a response. They finally emerged from the rear, smiling adamantly, their business apparently settled, and unapologetic for the delay they had caused. N'Djamé nodded to Cadere, who accompanied him back out of sight to the rear.

In a moment we heard the groan of Cadere opening the tin-clad gate to the street. The motor started, and the truck emerged with N'Djamé at the wheel and Cadere standing in the rear, holding onto the top. They stopped by the stoop, and Cadere brusquely directed the loading of Abdou Dieye and two others to whom N'Djamé had agreed to give rides. Young Gana consulted one last time at the window with N'Djamé, who listened impassively and interrupted to tell Cadere to hurry up. In short order the *apprentis* had finished his business. N'Djamé swung the truck in a wide arc and sped away to the north, past the peanut cooperative, disappearing behind the Sene compounds on his way to the road.

    The vacuum left in their wake was quickly filled by confusion from the charrette. Biran N'Dour had finally reappeared with a bulging burlap sack on his head, which he dropped into the rear of the charrette causing a sudden imbalance which startled the horse into frightened rearing. The women in the charrette screamed and clung to the sides, keeping their weight low and leaning forward as it tilted up at a severe angle. Old Gana and the others around the charrette fell away, and pandemonium reigned; but the driver finally stepped forward and managed to quiet his horse. There followed an argument between Biran and the driver about paying for the extra weight, with Biran eventually prevailing through sheer stubborn inertia.

    The charrette was now full and the horse quiet. After a few more minutes of rearranging the baggage and some final messages from bystanders, it jerked into motion and began the long trip in N'Djamé's tracks. Badiane called to Biran to keep an eye out for cheap chickens in the village of Yaye, two miles along the way, referring both to the fact that N'Djamé was infamous for running over chickens there and that Biran was well known for delaying whatever charrette he happened to be riding in order to barter for chickens on his own way to the road. As the charrette made its way steadily up towards the Sene compounds the clusters of people back at the boutique began to dissipate, with everyone eager to accomplish their various tasks before noon.

Old Gana came over and greeted Badiane and me, explaining that he had sent a message via the woman in the charrette to his second wife in her village near the road, and that he was planning to journey there himself. He spoke with gravity, as if such a journey were not so much a pleasure as part of the business of being a man. He and Badiane chatted briefly as peers; and then he left us, striding slowly back up to his own compound where the charrette had just disappeared.

Young Gana likewise greeted us, but his mind was bursting with the preparations he would have to accomplish before noon, and he soon bustled off towards his own boutique, where the *griots* continued their drumming. Badiane and I smiled to each other as we watched him leave. He shook his head and clucked a sound of knowing amazement at the frenzied state that Gana was in, and at the wheeling-dealing world of both him and N'Djamé.

"*Defa baré affaires* [he's too busy]," he said with benign disapproval, then translating confidentially: "*Il a trop de problèmes.*"

Badiane had once been a boutique-owner himself in another village, with three wives and a truck to his credit. His sons, it was said, had 'eaten' all his profits. He had been unable to maintain his vehicle, he had plunged quickly back into poverty, and all his wives had left him. He had later, he had told me, spent several years as an aide to some Lebanese hunters in various parts of Senegal. He spoke passable French and Arabic in addition to Wolof and Serrer. His worldly life behind him now, he lived as a cheerful bachelor on the edge of N'Dondol Oulof, cultivating modest amounts of peanuts and millet, growing his beloved manioc, and keeping his affairs in scrupulous order. He adhered closely to his Moslem beliefs and seemed to be successfully approximating the constantly-repeated ideal of *djam a-rek* [peace only].

I asked him now if he was going to attend the *réunion* [meeting] and he said that he was not going to do so—that he would go to his field and spend the noon hours under the shade of his mango tree.

We bade each other good day, and I turned up the street towards the well, passing between Biran N'Dour's tiny boutique and that of Tchekumba Sene, both of which were sheathed with flattened-out oil drums. Behind another tin shack which happened to be the village mosque sat Aliou N'Dao's unfinished cement house, whose crumbling bricks and rusting reinforcing bars gave it the appearance of a ruin. He had begun it two years earlier, but had not been able to amass enough money since to continue its construction. This was a common occurrence among heads of households who aspired to the permanence and prestige of a cement dwelling. A number of yards contained only crumbling piles of weatherworn bricks as testaments to their owners' stalled ambitions.

Although the region was predominantly and traditionally Serrer, this central portion of the village was composed of Wolof households, laid out in rectangles along a modest grid of sandy streets. Distinguished by a number of cement block, tin roof dwellings, it was referred to in the surrounding Serer compounds as the *dukaba* [town] or *tachyi* [cement buildings].

Outside of this nucleus of the Wolof establishment lay the households of artisan castes—*teugues* [blacksmiths], *gewels* [griots, musicians], and *laobés* [woodworkers]—and then the surrounding Serrer compounds. These were more organic in both layout and construction, incorporating fewer of the artifacts of industrial civilization. They were more fluid in their external boundaries, composed almost entirely of millet stalk, reeds and straw and sitting more intimately upon the land. Beyond them came typically an expanse of fields, and then, at a radial distance of two to three miles, a number of smaller Serrer villages, most of which depended on our village for their water.

Generally speaking, the Wolof had been quicker to adopt various elements of modernity into their lives, while the Serrer embraced their agrarian traditions. The Wolof adhered more adamantly to the tenets of Islam and were more deeply involved in a money economy, while the Serrer herded cattle and maintained their animist beliefs. The Serrer regarded the Wolof with suspicion for their preoccupation with money and politics; and the Wolof regarded the Serrer as unsophisticated farmers who had nonetheless to be respected because of their traditional knowledge. Almost all Serrer spoke Wolof, while very few Wolof spoke Serrer; and since neither was a written language, French remained the language of commerce and government in the world beyond the village.

I approached the central village well, which was called Nopili. If N'Djamé Sene's boutique was a commercial and political focal point of the village, Nopili was its spiritual center. It was now crowded with women, five or six of whom at a time stood at the lip drawing water from its 15 meter depths. I noticed a group from N'Diamane, a village several miles to the southeast, and waved to Gorgui Yatte's wife; but I gave the women my usual wide berth, not wanting to tangle with that many agile and aggressive tongues.

Behind them lay the village market place, a decrepit array of tattered shade roofs. According to the traditional market system, different villages hosted region-wide markets on different days. Our Monday market, which had apparently once been quite vigorous, had fallen into severe decline. During the dry season, when there was money in the area, it would succeed in drawing a modest crowd: A few charrettes would arrive from the surrounding countryside, a truck would come from M'Bour selling fish, and Mang N'Diaye, the butcher, would kill a goat or a cow. It still lacked the magnetism of others in the region, however, and at this time of year it lay destitute.

Leaving it and Nopili behind me I walked up a slight rise to the large expanse of sand where stood he village's edifices of modernity — buildings which had been constructed by the government to certify the entry of the village into a world where institutions were set apart from the rest of the fabric of life. To my right was the peanut cooperative, with its steel frame, tin-sheathed storage shed and its fenced-in yard for the seasonal massing of peanuts. To my left were the two schoolrooms, empty during this part of the year, and the little residence for the schoolteachers.

It was becoming more and more normal for the children of the village to attend school during the dry season, although more so for the Wolof than the Serrer. Instruction was in French, and the first task was to learn that language. One of the classes was taught by radio broadcast from Dakar, with the teachers assisting and supplementing the lesson. The students would attend the school for a number of seasons until they either passed the examination enabling them to attend the next level of school in a town or they abandoned their academic careers. A good number of sons and daughters of Wolofs attended secondary school elsewhere now and returned to the village only for vacations. Their continued education tended to move them into a different world from the village, one characterized by literacy and things French. For some the goal was now to get to France or, increasingly, America. Others retained a deep love for the village and wanted to serve it in some capacity. The chances for success in either case seemed to be remote because of the general level of poverty of the country; and these students existed in a kind of limbo, drawing further away from the village on a road which led nowhere.

Over to the left past the schoolrooms sat the Maison des Jeunes, frequented only by goats. Its porch roof sagged ominously, and birds were nesting under its tin eaves. Apparently governmental officials had had it built in preparation for a visit by the president of the country some ten years before. The president had arrived by helicopter, sending the women at the well into full-blown panic, and had been shown the building during his tour of the village. It had sat empty ever since.

Finally, on the northwest corner of this civic arena, sat the medical dispensary, with several women outside with their babies talking with the *infirmier's* wife. The little building consisted of two rooms — a treatment room and a residence room. It was in need of repairs, and bats squeaked constantly up in the roof.

When we had first arrived in the village the *infirmier* [trained nurse] had been a young man of western inclinations from near Dakar who was widely mistrusted and who longed to get back to the city. He had finally arranged for exchange of positions with an older Wolof man who worked in a hospital in Dakar and who wanted to retire to a peaceful life in the country. Diop, or *le docteur* as he was often called, had brought his wife and children with him; and *le dispensaire* now seemed more like a home. He had fenced the back, added a couple of thatch huts, tried his hand at growing peanuts beside the building, and turned the old defunct outhouse into a chicken coop. He was enjoying country life and was well accepted in the village, although he seldom actually had any medicine to dispense. He would give dehydrated babies a big injection of saline solution in their stomachs; and Thursday was leper day, when he would distribute free grain to those afflicted with that disease.

After Diop had been there a month the Wolof women had given his wife, Fall, a welcome dance; and there would normally be a group of women gossiping outside the building during the day. The Serrer women still tended to mistrust the place, however, as they did other intrusions into traditional life.

To my right lay the familiar compounds of N'Dondol Séssene, the major Serrer portion of the village, lying peaceful and quiet under their spreading trees. Outside of Modou Yatte's compound, Kodou Gning and Sey Dieng were sifting millet in the nearly still air, shaking it from gourds held above their heads and letting the chaff drift into a pile a few feet away while the grains fell onto a piece of cloth spread out at their feet.

The scene was idyllic, a picture-book image of Africa. Just a few days before a huge Gulf oil truck had sat against that same peaceful background, its great engine throbbing. The driver had been a cousin of one of the families up in the Diouf compounds and had a sweetheart there. With the sand of the trails more compact because of the rains he had managed to come north through the countryside from M'Bour to visit her on his way about his business. I had found myself among the crowd which had gathered in curiosity and awe. He had stayed for an hour, revving the engine proudly; and then he had left, rumbling off through the countryside between tightly flanking fields of millet.

The millet was halfway up, now. It had finally rained—not generously, but enough; and with its growth the physical experience of the countryside was changing. No longer did the land beyond our house lie exposed in naked panorama; it was covered now. In another month, when the millet surpassed human height, one would find oneself bracketed in a virtual maze of millet-blinded paths as one walked anywhere outside this periphery of the village. Now, one looked across waist-high seas of grain—seas which deteriorated badly in places, but seas nonetheless, whose waving surface betrayed the presence of breezes which never seemed to reach one in the blazing heat of the day.

A charrette was approaching now with three figures aboard, coming from M'Bomboye or parts beyond. Their connection to the ground obscured, they seemed to bob and buck to the vagaries of the waves of millet. They were lightly laden, and the horse was fast. I could distinguish Seidu Sall on the front bench, with his brother Papa driving beside him and Seidu's wife N'Dey Ba behind. They emerged from the sea of grain and decelerated jerkily to a stop beside me at my gate.

We greeted each other warmly and Seidu stepped down. He had on his best *bou-bou* [plain robe] of spotless beige cloth. Papa also wore a bou-bou and his customary sunglasses, and N'Dey was resplendent in a new *complête* [matching top, bottom, and kerchief] with a shawl of diaphanous green. With the drums calling from the other side of the village, Papa was impatient to continue on. After the briefest of chats he whipped his horse into motion and left us in their wake, with N'Dey waving regally from the rear. Seidu and I watched them disappear behind the cooperative and then went in the yard. The drums continued.

Seidu had lived in his father's household down on the edge of N'Dondol Oulof until recently. One day when we had been eating there the old man had announced to his family in a formal speech that they were moving to his second household in M'Bomboye. I was never quite certain of the circumstances behind the move, but in one respect it constituted an abandonment of city ambitions. Their compound out in M'Bomboye, sitting alone on the savannah, had an air of relaxed, spacious grandeur which their place in the relatively crowded center of the village had never achieved. The latter was empty now, the lock of the gate securing some decaying thatch huts, a large pile of crumbling cement bricks, and Seidu's father's old rusting automobile.

Seidu and his family were Toucouleur, a people living generally farther to the north who under their great leader El Hadji Omar had been the last to present the French with significant armed resistance. They were known as an extremely proud people. I was not certain what circumstances had led to the family's living among the Serrer and Wolof; they were the only Toucouleur whom I knew in the area except for N'Dey's family, whom I had met once in the village of Talegne four miles away.

Seidu had gone to primary school in Dakar when he was younger, and he spoke good French. He was employed by the government now as a *vulgarizateur* [agricultural outreach worker] in a program which seemed to be the most successful of the various extensions of the government to the people of the countryside. He and Guedj Sene were assigned to N'Dondol and its surrounding ring of smaller villages. Following a regular schedule, they would walk each day to a different village and talk with the people there about farming methods, about fertilizers, and so forth. They were diligent, they were well respected, they were of the village; and their work contrasted favorably with the government programs which depended on *fonctionaires* from the town of Bambey, 15 miles away, making expeditions *en brousse* at unpredictable intervals.

Seidu cared very deeply about the future of the village—about its ability to benefit from western knowledge without losing its cultural bearings. He also had a boundless sense of humor which rescued him from the depths of utter frustration with the often-farcical relationship between the government and the people, and with the many mis-steps of a culture in uncertain transition. He would entertain us with imitations of his *patron* in Bambey, eloquent and impassioned examples of what he, Seidu, should have said to him on such-and-such an occasion, or parodies of the oratorical styles of both village and governmental officials. Before any given meeting he could predict exactly what would be said—which was a lot—and exactly what would result from it—which was usually nothing.

When N'Dey had been pregnant the previous year he had taken her to Bambey to have the baby at the maternity there. This was something which was unheard of for a villager, but Seidu felt that it befit his station to do so—in part as a demonstration of modern methods—and his *patron* had encouraged it and assured him that the government would cover the expenses.

N'Dey had given birth to a healthy little girl there with no complications and after a few days had returned to the village with her. Ever since then, however, Seidu had been running in circles trying to get the government to reimburse him. He would find some free time, pay *car-rapide* fare to Thies, and present his bills and *carte d'identité* at the appropriate office; and the people there would send him back to Bambey to get a special authorization signature from his superior. This he would secure, and then find time to go to Thies again only to be sent to Diourbel for a special form from somewhere else; and then on his next expedition to Thies he would find that someone in Bambey had not mailed a crucial piece of paper, forcing him to go back to Bambey only to find that the official in Thies had in fact simply mislaid the piece of paper.

This had gone on for so long that it was beginning to seem plausible that he would literally never secure the reimbursement which he had been promised; and the amount of money he had had to spend on car fare and special fees was becoming quite considerable. But Seidu was indefatigable, and through a mixture of pride and need never ceased to believe that the system would ultimately give him what he sought. He would arrive in our yard, slump in our hammock, recount the latest charade in which he had participated, sinking to the lowest ebb of his spirit, and then burst forth with a hilarious and purgative parody of the pomposity of governmental officialdom.

Today, Seidu had stopped by to spend the late morning before the occasion which the drums had been announcing since sunrise and which was scheduled to start at noon. We sat under the shade roof in the front yard sharing cigarettes, munching the inevitable *guru*, and reviewing between ourselves and various friends who dropped by, the recent political events of the village.

The issue between the people and the government was always money, which was always scarce. The forces of progress and modernization were pressuring the people slowly into a money economy, tending to move them from a state of self-sufficiency to a state of poverty. The farmers' only source of income was their crop of peanuts, a monoculture instituted by the French, whose price had been falling steadily on the world market and which were poor these years in any case. The government, on its part, had inherited from the French a dense bureaucracy on which a growing educated class depended for their livelihood. It was a poor country, with little to barter with the rest of the world. The government had a hard enough time supporting itself, let alone fulfilling its promises of service to the people. The perspective of the village was very simple: The government simply did not do enough to justify its periodic intrusion into their lives.

Earlier this rainy season affairs between them had brewed to a head over the issue of debts which the people owed the government for seed and fertilizer borrowed the previous year. The crop had been a poor one, and the villagers felt that it was unfair to be expected to repay with the little money they had received, especially since the loan program had been initiated by the government to begin with. The government, however, had decided to launch a strenuous effort to collect all outstanding debts. The burden, then, had fallen upon the *préfet* of Bambey to come out to the village and put pressure on the people; and he had done so in a series of meetings.

Most everyone reluctantly came across with peanuts or money or even millet, but a few claimed that they had no money and refused to pay with their families' food. Finally, the *préfet* announced a deadline of noon on a particular day when he would appear with *gendarmes* to remove the holdouts to jail in Bambey. When the day arrived he was true to his word; and Saliou Diouf, Maury Dia, and M'Baye Gadjiaga were taken away.

Stories of beating and torture circulated through the village: It was known to have happened in the past, and it was expected to be happening now. There was much talk and carrying-on throughout the village, and young Gana went to Bambey to plead with officials; but the three men remained in jail. Finally, after three days, N'Djamé Sene, who had designs on becoming chief, drove to Bambey, paid the men's debts, and brought them back to the village in triumph. Saliou had immediately scrounged the money to repay N'Djamé, thus undermining the man's role as a hero among the Serrer; but a power struggle was nonetheless now underway between N'Djamé and young Gana.

The two men had once been fast friends, sharing the pinnacle of the local prestige ladder. Gana was a Serrer from Séssene who had become the first chief of the entire village through a combination of high standing among the important Serrer matrilineages, wealth from his boutique, and political connections which he had established beyond the village. He had learned to read and write French, was the *peseur* [weigher] at the Cooperative, and was a representative to the Conseil Regional at Diourbel. At the height of his prestige he had befriended N'Djamé, a Serrer from M'Bomboye who spoke only Wolof and was not well accepted by either group. He had staked him to money to get a start in commerce, and N'Djamé's star had risen rapidly. With his wealth had come acceptance and support, and he had accumulated four wives, to match Gana in that category.

During the month following the debt-collection incident N'Djamé could be seen conferring with prominent Wolofs such as Abdou Dieye and Mademba N'Diaye, and an open rift developed between him and Gana. The latter, meanwhile, seemed to be treading water frantically. His money had leaked away because of his obligation to distribute largesse and to support a retinue as a manifestation of his high standing and because his political life kept him too busy to keep up his boutique; and he was openly rumored to be cheating at the Cooperative, siphoning off money to cover his debts and engaging in disastrous wheeling and dealings which sent him deeper and deeper into financial chaos. He had long ago abandoned his automobile, his boutique was bare, and his kerosene refrigerator no longer worked. He could no longer compete with N'Djamé in the purchasing of support. Remaining in his favor were the tribal loyalty of the Serrer, his political connections beyond the village, and a certain amount of personal charisma which N'Djamé lacked.

As time passed Gana grew increasingly frantic, while N'Djamé grew more self-confident. Matters finally came to a head with N'Djamé appealing to government officials to help bring about the change of leadership which he felt he could demonstrate that the people wanted. Gana emerged with his position intact, however, by enlisting the active support of the mayor of Bambey, the most powerful political personage in the whole area. The mayor came out to the village for a public réunion and appealed to N'Djamé and Gana to abandon their feud; and this pressure was enough to deflate N'Djamé's power move.

The two had become reconciled rather quickly, at least for the time being. One evening not long afterwards N'Djamé's truck had roared past our gate and Bity had smiled, saying that it was Gana and N'Djamé going out to M'Bomboye to *wouti jabbar* [look for wives]. There was some speculation now that N'Djamé would retire from the political arena of the village and seek to become chief of one of the portions of M'Bomboye.

Now when old Gana—young Gana's uncle—had been chief many years before, an incident similar to this debt-collection episode had occurred, the result of which had been that officials in Bambey had demanded his surrender and that of several other Serrer. There had been much debate in the village about whether and how to force or avoid the issue. Gana had said that the nature of his power was such that if he worked certain magic no jail could hold him or anyone in his company. He proceeded to march with the others to Bambey and into the office of the official in question, citing the man's lineage and his own, saying that he had known the man's father and his father's father and demanding what it was that he wanted of them. The man looked at him and said "Go back to your village, Gana Sene—I cannot hold you here"; and the Serrers returned to the village the same day.

Old Gana had apparently been the last purely tribal chief of the Serrers of the village. Later, when local power structures had been altered by the French and their appointees, the entire village had become defined as a single political entity; and young Gana had become the first chief of this combined entity, both Wolof and Serrer. While this was a formidable accomplishment, it also seemed to mark a sea change in the power structure of the region. It seemed to us that power had now become desacralized— that young Gana's power now had much more to do with wealth and external political connections than whatever combination of traditional legitimacy, personal presence, and magic had enabled old Gana to stare down the Bambey officials.

Young Gana as we knew him seemed to be a pure politician, working ceaselessly to maintain his position, to counterbalance and keep at bay the countless pressures and demands upon him. He spent his days either outside his empty boutique in the Wolof portion of the village, besieged by a retinue of retainers, favor seekers, and the like, or behind closed doors with select people at either his Oulof or Séssene residence, or at the Cooperative where he was the focus of a whole other and even more intense nexus of people and concerns. He often retreated to our house from the Cooperative for a half-hour's respite from his problems. He would slump in a hammock under the shade roof sipping cool water from our cement *ndah* and swear over and over again that it was the coolest place in the entire village, and that all that was important in life was *djam a-rek* [peace only].

During the N'Djamé affair his nerves had grown worse. His speech constantly darted off on tangents; his mind was never still. Sometimes we would hear him down at the Cooperative at night directing some massive shuffle of peanuts from one place to another; and the next day Bity would try to explain to us what the latest bit of wheeling, dealing, compensation and cover-up was all about. His position came increasingly under siege, his empire into more and more imminent danger of disintegration. I discovered him one day, when he thought it was someone else at his door, holding a pistol in his hands and musing to himself. Even at home in Séssene he had little peace, as one or another of his four wives was always going home to her mother's compound amid great domestic turmoil, requiring tedious negotiations to lure here back.

At bottom all young Gana seemed to want in his affairs was *djam a-rek*; but every new exertion seemed to take him farther away from that goal. He was charting a new course in a world which each day was further removed from that of his ancestors; and through prodigious, taxing effort he was at least holding his own.

Old Gana, by contrast, was living out his life in the world of the old Serrers. He was a respected elder, he was lord of his compound, he kept his diminishing affairs in good order; but he simply did not live in the world which had been opened up to young Gana. In Séssene, by the cook fires, among the compounds and trees he had known all his life he was still a powerful figure: His body was still strong, his hands and feet like great bludgeons, his one good eye bright and gleaming, his presence patriarchal. Down *chi tachyi*, in the Wolof portion of the village, he was an old man whose time was past.

His preoccupation now was *bane-bane* [petty trade]. He would supervise his domain in Séssene, having Bity plough his field and M'Baye Tchiao tend his horse, working once in a while, making rope with the bark stripped from his trees, making water bags from old inner tubes, selling leaves of tobacco to old Serrers who didn't want to patronize the Wolof boutiques, visiting and being visited, until he got the urge to travel. Then one night when we ate his wife Tchab's *tcheré* we would hear him inside his *neg* getting his bags together, grating up *gurus* into a little tin for the journey, dispatching Bity or Modou N'Gom off to some remote Serrer compound to collect a bag a millet or a couple of chickens which were owed to him; and then the next day he would be off to Dakar to trade his goods until he ended up with more tobacco, some old inner tubes, and just enough money to make it back to the village. Once in a great while he would visit his second wife in her village near the road: He would rumble past our gate on his charrette, magnificent in his deep blue grand *bou-bou*, looking like the right hand of God as he whistled the whip at his horse's ear.

The drums which had been calling since morning were heralding what was the culmination of the latest crisis in the relationship between the government and the village. At noon the governor of the entire region (there were seven regions in the country) was scheduled to arrive, the most eminent political presence to set foot in the village in many years, to provide an official statement on the issue of inscription in the national political party.

As usual, the government wanted money from the people, and as usual the people wanted money from the government. In the wake of general anger and resistance to the debt-collection efforts the government had eventually announced a cancellation of all outstanding debt; but now it had launched a drive to boost Party membership and collect the associated inscription fees.

Party membership had once been high, especially among the Serrer of the countryside who were proud that one of their own was president of the country; but it had fallen off in recent years among these very people among whom the president's party claimed strong support. The current drive was apparently going reasonably well in the region as a whole, but extraordinarily poorly in our area.

The people, for their part, were asking for an advance on the money they were to be paid for their current crop of peanuts, as the month of Ramadan with its feast of Korité was fast approaching. The government was maintaining that the recent cancellation of outstanding tax and loan debts was enough of a concession and that the people should now demonstrate their good faith by inscribing unanimously in the Party.

The new *préfet* — the old one having been removed in the wake of the debt-collection episode — had visited the village a month earlier, expressing dismay at the low Party membership, especially among the Serrer. There had been much powerful oratory on that occasion, and the rallying cry of *"cent pourcent!"* [one hundred percent!] had rung from every village chief's lips; but a week, and two weeks, and three weeks later there had been only a token increase in inscriptions.

Young Gana was caught in the middle, as usual, with anger rising on both sides of him. The government was now wary of using force, as the situation in the countryside was considered volatile, and had decided upon the visitation by *Le Governeur* as a show of magnificence without an explicit physical threat.

As so the reunion was scheduled for noon today, and Gana was frantic with the task of making arrangements. The *griots* were already drumming; Sobel N'Gom of N'Diamane would be there to sing; Dembl Faye, a heralded blind singer from a village near M'Bah Faye, would be there; and of course nearly everyone within a radius of two to three miles would be there in their best *grand bou-bous* and finery.

A table had been set up under one of three huge spreading *bentenyi* trees where the path left the village towards N'Diedieng near Ibraima Gning's little boutique, a spot providing a maximum of shaded open space. Gana had sent messengers to round up every available chair in the village for the comfort of important personages.

All of this was quite normal for a political réunion, simply done with more intensity and excitement. What was unusual was the meal, which Gana had planned for the governor, after endless consideration and discussion. Ordinarily the fare would be the very best meal possible in Serrer or Wolof style, the food they would prepare for themselves at their own most important baptisms, funerals, and feasts. This would consist of great kettles of *tcheb-u-djen, tcheb-u-yappe, yassa, mafi* or whatever, served to groups in large gourds on the ground and eaten with the hand. These were magnificent occasions; and only at these times did many of the Serrer enjoy the rich pleasure of eating rice or palm oil or meat.

For *Le Gouverneur*, however, Gana was planning a *toubab's* meal of meat, fried potatoes, and salad to be eaten off of tin plates with utensils. And the crowning touch was to be mayonnaise. The word had reached Gana that the governor was fond of mayonnaise; and Gana had been stockpiling eggs from our chickens—felt to be superior to ordinary village chicken eggs because we had bought them at a hatchery in Thies— to make great bowls of mayonnaise. This would be the *pièce de résistance* for what was already certain to be a splendid occasion. The site of the reunion was even now being festooned with bunting which Gana had obtained in advance from officials in Bambey; and as a unique and flamboyant touch there was to be a group of riders who would wait for the governor's fleet *en route* and gallop before them into the village, the lead pair carrying Senegalese flags.

Sitting in our hammocks reviewing the situation Seidu and I were becoming impatient. Because it was the norm for official visitors to arrive late, we planned to delay at least until noon before walking down under the sun to the site of the réunion; but the drums had been tugging at the backs of our minds all morning until it had become extremely difficult to stay away. N'Djamé's truck had already roared past Séssene on its return to his boutique; a messenger from young Gana had long ago collected the last of our eggs; another had taken our two chairs; and various of our friends from Séssene had already stopped by and then departed for the réunion.

Aliou Diouf was sitting with us now, joining in the conversation, and M'Baye Tchiao, who had malaria, was leaning silently against the porch. Nini was in Dakar; and Bity was off on an errand for this father, collecting a portion of a particular vine that the old man had noticed growing three miles away on the other side of Yaye.

Old Gana himself came in at the gate now, carrying a water bag which we had commissioned to replace our worn one. He demonstrated the superiority of his own method of sewing the rubber; and I paid him for it.

"*Dinga wali te* [Will you attend today]?" I asked him, gesturing towards the drums. The old man had little tolerance for modern politics and disapproved of young Gana's complicated affairs.

"*Dina wali kai* [Certainly, I'll attend]," he assured me, "*Dina wali, waya duma fa yag.* [I'll attend, but I won't stay long]." He implied that the occasion demanded his presence but could not hold it for long.

"*Gis nga, Fall,*" he said now shaking his head with disapproval,

"Gouni-yi denyu booga yak dukabi, dugadugadug: Denyu booga yak reo-mi lip. [The youngsters are going to ruin the village, that's the truth: They're going to ruin the whole country]." Leaving us with that gloomy assessment, he bade us good day and headed back towards Séssene.

"Maggot bo-bou [That old one]," said Aliou gesturing towards his departing figure, *"Am-on ne doli. Ki kay mome, am-on ne doli lol* [He used to have power. He really, really used to have some power]."

"Wackh nga dug, kai [You speak the truth]," Seidu commented, shaking his head with reverence: *"Wackh nga dugadugadug."*

We passed on to further discussion of the *réunion*, with Seidu explaining that none of the village speakers would dare to confront the governor with grievances because they couldn't afford official reputations as troublemakers and because traditional form called for the speaking of *djam a-rek*. He said that the chiefs knew what they ought to say if the confrontation were to be anything more than a formal charade, but that when the time came for them to speak they would be swept up into their pre-ordained roles in the drama and would deliver tremendous orations signifying absolutely nothing.

Towards noon the drums grew louder as the young *griots* were joined by their elders, and their pull finally became too strong to be denied. We walked across the field past the schoolrooms and the Cooperative in the hot, draining sun, down past the well, through the Wolof portion of the village and out the other side to the shade of the spreading *bentenyis* where a considerable crowd had gathered.

The central area was clear of people, with the *griots* on one side of the circle and a table and chairs listing at various angles in the sand on the other side. The trees and fences were draped with bunting in the familiar green, red, and yellow of the Senegalese flag. On the center of the table had been placed sprigs of *basi*, the most beautiful of the three strains of millet, and several handfuls of peanuts—all from the previous year's crops.

Young Gana was presiding in all his glory, resplendent in a *grand bou-bou* of light brown material with gold embroidery, smiling broadly and directing the whirlwind about him with ceaseless energy. Several of the chiefs of neighboring villages were there and seated: Waly Gueye of N'Gouye, Assane Saar of M'Bomboye I, Joby Thiao of M'Bomboye II, Soona Tchiam of Wachaldjam, and Lamane N'Gom of N'Diedieng I, all impressively attired in their best robes. Near them and Gana stood a number of prominent Wolof: Abdou Dieye, Moussa Dieye, Mademba N'Diaye and others—like everyone, abuzz with the excitement of the occasion. I noticed N'Djamé Sene on the edge of the cluster of important personages, wearing a beautiful emerald green *grand bou-bou* but appearing somewhat self-conscious and shy.

I pushed through the crowd to the center, carefully greeted each man and chatted briefly with those I knew well, politely evaded Gana's insistence that I take a chair, and retreated to the edge of the circle next to Aliou to watch the show.

The inner edge of the circle consisted mostly of children, with grown women standing behind them in costume of infinite variety. There was N'Dey Ba in her diaphanous green, giggling when our eyes met across the circle; and there was N'Djoli Dia laughing with her friend Fatou Dia and her sister Soda; there were two of Gana's wives; and there were two of N'Djamé's; and there was a whole group of young griot women shrieking and jittering with excitement.

There was Fatou N'Diaye, immense and dignified, behind a covey of her brother Yibou's children; and Awa Fall, and Amy Lay, and dozens of others. Amongst and behind them stood equal numbers of men, Serrer and Wolof, of all castes, from all the villages, their generally plain, sober *bou-bous* outshone by the women's bright attire. The place was filling up fast. I sat cross-legged in the sand, dug a *guru* out of my pocket and shared it with Aliou beside me, and waited for the dancing to begin.

Cadere Dia had been appointed to keep the crowd back. He was a perfect choice for the job, a prime example of Wolof genius in human management. The situation was this: You had a crowd of people in a state of high emotional excitement whose irrepressible tendency was to surge towards the center as their excitement increased; and you had a need for a sizeable open space in the middle for the principal participants in the drama to play their parts. The perimeter had to be maintained if the great organism of the réunion was not to suffocate of its own enthusiasm, but in some manner which did not deflate that excitement or prevent it from developing. The solution was to give a notoriously mean and tough man a short loud whip and direct him to lash the sand at the crowd's edge to move them back when they surged too close. Cadere was ideal for this. He had no qualms about whipping close to people; and those at the edge of the crowd, understanding this, would recede reflexively as he approached, regarding him as one does an incoming wave as one stands at the water's edge in dry clothes. The result was a way of maintaining the perimeter in an elastic fashion, allowing it to pulsate with the ebb and flow of emotional electricity in the crowd.

Excitement was already beginning to mount—the dancing would surely begin soon—and Cadere was beginning to ease slowly into his task. Gana was standing by the table clutching Badara D'Diaye by the shoulders, dispatching him on some urgent errand even as he turned to grope into the crowd for yet another messenger. M'Baye Diouf, the head of one family of *griots*, black as coal with hands which would be sore and swollen the next day, took over the biggest drum from his son and immediately pushed the intensity of the music up several notches. The rhythm became muddled momentarily as the six or seven drummers struggled to keep up with him; and then the new pattern burst forth with such power that a young girl shot into the center as if plucked from the crowd. She danced for perhaps five seconds and then plunged giggling back to her place with her friends as another girl burst from the crowd across the circle to take her place.

This pattern continued as the crowd began to focus on the dancers. Shouts of "No children! Keep the children out!" were heard from men who wanted to dispense with giggling childishness on such an occasion; but this beginning was inevitable, providing the first, tentative movement of the emotional cycle of the dance.

The fire of arousal flared fitfully for a while as various children danced. Sometimes two would run out at the same time and interfere with each other, calming the flame; and sometimes a particularly poised girl would be able to draw it out, to fan it, to establish a communication between herself and the drummers.

A lull of about a minute fell over the scene, and as the intensity rebuilt, it was apparent that a new phase had been reached. A young woman was dancing now, her body more mature, her control more authoritative. The crowd came alive; the drumming quickened. She was replaced by another, as good, and then another who was even better. The crowd pressed forward; Cadere went to work. A beautiful young *griot* woman stepped into the circle now and had the self-possession to pause and stare at the drummers, challenging them to do better; and they quickly developed an exchange between them which built to a new peak. The crowd shrieked with approval, and the dancer continued.

I heard a voice in my ear: *"Ki munult fetch* [This one can't dance]," it said, betraying a mixture of jealousy and contempt. It was N'Djémi Faye, Bity's *djourbat* [child of his sister], one of the best dancers among the Serrer women.

"Aitcha bok," I challenged; and she smiled. She would wait a while yet to make sure that she wasn't associated with the children. She was proud, and took her dancing seriously.

After two more women the drummers stopped, taking the first of several breaks they would take during the mature phase of the dance. I shifted my legs and looked around. I had not noticed how hot it had become; and I was getting thirsty. I took out another half of a *guru* and shared it with Aliou and N'Djémi. Almost everyone had by now arrived. Gana had attained an emotional plateau and was actually seated, smiling broadly, allowing himself a brief moment of satisfaction with the occasion taking place around him. He was visibly *'borom dukaba'* [lord of the village], and all was in place for the arrival of the governor.

In the background behind the chiefs and political personages stood a group of Serrer elders, among whom, was old Gana. Further around the circle from them stood Saliou Diouf, impressive in his best *bou-bou*, but decidedly on the outskirts. Next to him stood Seidu, impassive and proud behind the women and children. His face broke into a grin as he shared a joke with Saliou. Almost everyone had arrived. Here and there on the outer edge of the circle stood a Serrer farmer, in working clothes with gop in hand, looking in with curiosity.

Now arrived an entourage from N'Diamane, the only distinct group which I had noticed to be missing. There was considerable commotion in order to give Sobel N'Gom and his cohorts a place at the edge of the circle. Gorgui Yatte, the young chief, began greeting Gana and the other chiefs before taking his place among them. His brother Saliou drifted to the rear near Seidu and Saliou Diouf. I went over to greet and chat with Gorgui, inquiring about his sick father; and then as the *griots* recommenced I returned to my place in the sand.

The drumming quickly returned to the pitch at which it had left off, and the dancing became more accomplished—hypnotic and erotic—with the dancers staying in the circle for longer durations of time. N'Djémi knelt between Aliou and me now, her hands on our shoulders ready to propel herself into the ring. We pretended to try to throw her in and she resisted, laughing. She was radiant—focused totally on the dance. Abdou Dieye's daughter was in there now, a fine dancer, coaxing the *griots* a little higher, the crowd a little tighter; and as she moved to leave, N'Djémi pushed off of our shoulders and into the middle, her timing perfect.

She seemed suspended over one spot in the sand, her legs, buttocks, shoulders and trailing arm each catching the pulse of a different drum and increasing the intensity of each while some point in her abdomen remained motionless. She kept it up longer than anyone else had, stretching the tattoo of the drums tighter and tighter until it seemed unsustainable. Her dancing was less heavily erotic than the woman before her, but more beautiful, more alive, more exciting. The crowd pressed in upon her; and the sound of Cadere's whip was lost in their screams. Finally the tension broke: Her feet returned to the sand, and she walked back to her friends behind us in triumph as another woman burst into the arena.

As she and the next woman danced the peak which had been reached slowly slipped away, and it became clear that N'Djémi had ruled the set. After a few more dancers, a few lesser peaks, the drummers took another break.

The spell broken, I looked up and surveyed the scene with a critical eye. The physical discomfort of heat and thirst and cramped legs wept over me like a wave. I shifted positions and remembered *Le Gouverneur*.

Impatience and a sense of waste decayed the glow which remained from the dance.

"*Ana gouverneur-bi?*" I asked Aliou with rhetorical outrage; and he reassured me with the inevitable "*Leygi mu nyo* [He's coming right now]," obviously caring very little whether great man showed up or not. He scrubbed his teeth with the soft fibrous end of a stick, which he kept in his pocket.

I looked around: The place was abuzz; the occasion was ripe. Everyone seemed happy and in their place. Only young Gana exhibited any anxiety. He was out of his seat once again and dispatching Badara N'Diaye on yet another urgent task.

Aliou and I lit cigarettes and talked about the dance. I was impatient for Sobel to start singing; and Aliou assured me that he would do so "*Leygi, leygi rek*." He pointed out blind Dembl Faye, whom I had never seen before. He looked like some sort of bizarre bird, with dark glasses and hair that was brushed up into a sharp ridge which ran from the middle of his forehead straight back. I asked if he was really as fine a singer as everyone had told me, and Aliou replied that he was better even than that.

"*Sobel mo co duk* [Sobel is better than him]," said N'Djémi with knowledgeable assurance behind us; and the drummers began again.

This next set was as powerful as had been the last, with N'Djémi dancing again along with several others who were her equals. The *griots* had gradually replenished their ranks and were proving themselves to be tireless.

During the next break I saw N'Djome Faye, who was to have been one of the riders in the governor's escort. He told me that they had abandoned the idea after about an hour of waiting outside the village listening to the drums and wanting to join the dance. Someone said that the great man wasn't going to come at all because officials were known, with good reason, to be scared of the magic of Serrers this far out in the countryside. I maintained that he couldn't possibly fail to live up to his commitment. The man agreed; Aliou shrugged; and the dancing began once again.

Older women were dancing now, many with babies on their backs. Their movements were heavier, fuller, with less frenzy but more seasoned erotic power. The babies seemed welded to their mothers by a force stronger than the swatch of material which bound them. They pressed the sides of their little heads tight against their mothers' backs, riding out all the motions of the dance in intimate union.

There was a false arrival alarm, but it caused little disruption. My mind submerged once more into the hot stew of the moment. The sand imprinting itself against my legs, the flies on my arms, the taste of *guru* at the back of my mouth, the dryness of my throat, the smell of hot air and sand and bodies, all merged into a single state of being which transcended either comfort or discomfort, massaged by the eddies and currents of the music and focused on the dancer in the center. Once again Le Gouverneur receded to the faint periphery of my consciousness to join thoughts of money and politics, of the afternoon slipping away, and of mayonnaise going bad in the African heat.

During the next break the entire locus of the celebration, including table and chairs, was shifted in order to keep it in the shade. Confusion reigned for a time, but all parts of the whole sorted themselves out as the drumming resumed. Aliou and I had to banish some children to regain our position at the front. The dance continued, and the next time my mind surfaced old Moussane Diouf was dancing, somewhat stiffer and more dignified than the younger women, easing her body through timeworn motions and shaking her bracelets like dry leaves. As I marveled at her grace I realized that an entire course had been run—that at least three hours had gone by. Young Gana was nowhere to be seen. Old Gana looked like he was leaving. The ceremonial peanuts on the table had been reduced to a pile of shells.

The dance ended, and Sobel and his companions began setting themselves up for their portion of the program. The young *griots* rested their drums in the sand. I rose and wandered around the site of the dance, nodding to friends, feeling bewildered. Young Gana was consulting with some people over towards his boutique. I greeted them and asked him if he had heard anything.

"*Leygi mu nyo,*" he said with his serene, all-encompassing smile: "*Leygi rek mu nyo.*"

I found Seidu, who had some water with him, and I drank eagerly. We laughed with some disgust about the situation, and he launched into an earnest explanation of how the officials' tardiness typified their attitude towards the people. I told him I wished someone would tell that to *Le Gouverneur*; and he agreed, but assured me that none would do so.

Sobel and his fellow singers were beginning to warm up along with the *griots*. I asked Seidu if it was true that the officials were hesitant to come out to the village because of Serrer magic. He said that it was true, but that the governor was surely going to show up nonetheless. He said that there were compounds in the countryside on this side of the village that I didn't know about which officials would under no circumstances visit and which he himself, a Toucouleur, bypassed on his daily rounds. He assured me as he had many times before, breaking into French to emphasize his point and to keep from being overheard, that there were things in these parts that I would be better off not to be curious about. Some of the old Serrers, he said, had *"tres bonnes têtes."* We talked of other things, and when Sobel finally started to sing we turned back to the circle of people.

The dancing started all over again, this time with a three-way oscillation set up between the dancer, the drummers, and the singers. Several men danced this time, led off by Djagar Djione, a wild old *griot* man.

Finally, during a break, as the table was being moved once again, the sound of automobile horns was heard approaching. Pandemonium swept the arena as a fleet of Land Rovers roared up and came to a halt in a huge cloud of dust. The *griots* drummed frenetically in welcome, and a large portion of the circle swarmed forth to meet the guests as they emerged from their cars.

The visiting party consisted of a couple of *gendarmes*, several Bambey officials whom I already knew, a number of young men whom I took to be assistants to the governor, the drivers, and several others, any one of whom could have been the great man himself. Except for three women from Bambey, who were in traditional dress, and several young men in French clothes, they all wore plain-cut, vaguely military suits of khaki or olive green—the one or two who might be the governor having a few decorations on their chests.

I greeted the group from Bambey, who introduced me to some of the lesser members of the entourage as young Gana ushered the most select group to the table to meet the chiefs. In a remarkably short time the major introductions had been accomplished and all were seated, some of the Serrer chiefs having now to stand because of the shortage of chairs. The music recommenced in earnest.

First Sobel sang, with various men and women taking their turns dancing; and then Dembl Faye sang his first set. The odd-looking blind man, one hand at his ear in order to hear his own voice in the din, was led slowly about the arena by a companion, screaming erratically in a high-pitched voice. I couldn't understand the words, and he seemed not to be able to get together with the drummers. I saw Bity and asked him if the singing was any good, and he said that it was terrible, that Dembl was not yet warmed up.

During the next break one of the young members of the governor's entourage to whom I had been introduced motioned me over to him. I was surprised, but assumed that he had been talking with some of the people from Bambey and wanted to ask me about the work I had been doing in the village. I squatted by his chair, we shook hands again, and he said in French that he understood that I owned a tape recorder and wondered if I had any blank tapes which I might give to him. I explained politely that I did not, and our conversation ended. I returned to my place.

For about an hour longer Sobel and Dembl traded sets, with the latter finally coordinating with the *griots* while producing an extraordinarily piercing barrage of song which Bity certified as pleasing.

Sobel and his chorus, for their part, performed with their customary élan an original song in Wolof praising the president of Senegal for the progress he had brought to the county:

"*Ecole bangi Senegal* [There is education in Senegal]

Ana cou co indi? [Who is it that brought it?]

Khana Senghor! [Was it not Senghor!]

Auto [the automobile] *bangi Senegal*

Ana cou co indi?

Khana Senghor!"

Khalis [money] *mangi Senegal…*

Usines [factories] *yangi Senegal…*"

Le Gouverneur, a small, thin, oldish man, received the song and the dancing with a hint of a smile. Gana beamed beside him like the director of a play sitting beside a critic on opening night. Finally the drums fell silent, and a flurry of commotion and consultation at the table signaled the beginning of the political portion of the reunion.

The meeting began with a piece of governmental protocol as Sakho, the appropriate *fonctionaire* from Bambey, stood facing the governor and read aloud, in French, a long description of the attributes of the village and its people. He spoke fluently and swiftly, with what I interpreted as a mixture of pride in performing his task well and embarrassment that it was clearly of little interest to *Le Gouverneur* and incomprehensible to the villagers.

I suddenly wondered if perhaps the governor himself might address the village in French. I realized that the visual component of the scene — the *fonctionaire* suits, the chiefs, the women in their finery and the national flags against the village background — was very familiar; that I had seen it many times before in news photographs of African politics. It had a totally different meaning to me now; and yet I was still uncertain of what was really going on in the hearts and minds of the participants.

I looked at Gorgui Yatte, the young Serrer chief of the village of N'Diamane, and tried to imagine what the occasion meant to him. Gorgui's grandfather had resisted the French and lived to see them subjugate the land; his father had seen his countrymen inherit the apparatus of colonialism, led by a Serrer to whom he referred with tribal pride by his first name; and now Gorgui himself was struggling to be an effective leader of his people, walking to Nini's class three times a week during the dry season just to try to learn how to read and write. His grandfather and young Gana's grandfather had been so close that it was said that the one could sit in N'Diamane with a flame in his hand and light the other's pipe two miles away; but now he and Gana were at odds, the latter swept up in his maelstrom of current day politics while he himself struggled just to keep pace.

What did it mean to be Gorgui Yatte, caught in the tension between a storied past and an uncertain future? What did it mean to him to have to trek to our village to engage in a public charade with *Le Gouverneur*, and to have to listen to Sakho address the man in French? What ran through Sakho's mind as he read his report in front of the uncomprehending gathering? And what was going on in the mind of that eminent personage himself, sitting there so small with that hint of a smile, in a cushioned chair in the sand of this remote village in the now-waning afternoon heat?

There commenced now a long series of orations by various chiefs and important persons, the form of which was magnificent, and the content of which merged to one in my mind. Yilliman N'Gom of Yaye set the pace with a lengthy impassioned speech whose message was that the previous year had been bad, the current year wasn't much better, and there was no money in the village. The government, he said, should let the matter of inscriptions rest until after the harvest, at which time everyone would surely join *"cent pourcent"*; and in the meantime it should distribute through the Cooperative an advance on the money it would be paying for the peanuts, in time for the upcoming feast of Korité. He started very slowly, greeting everyone, saluting everyone, praising everyone, building steadily up to the heart of his oration which he delivered at the top of his voice, and then coming down gracefully to a conclusion, again praising everyone present and hoping for *"djam a-rek!"*

This basic form was followed by everyone. The speeches were as beautiful, as exciting, as similar, and as different as had been the dances of the women earlier. Abdou Dieye spoke with a hint of slyness; Mademba N'Diaye gave an impression of failing strength; Joby Tchiao nearly bowled over the assembly with an explosive oration; Gorgui Yatte spoke with energetic sincerity although faltering and falling short of the oratorical grandeur of the more experienced speakers; and several others took their turns before Gana sealed it all with a smooth, conciliatory, host-like offering.

There was now a brief statement of acknowledgement and appreciation on behalf of the official delegation by a man described to me as the *gouverneur-adjuant*; and we awaited the pronouncements of the governor himself.

There remained one more prefatory piece of oratory, however. An important member of the official party, it developed, was a *griot* named Fall, who now delivered the most exciting piece of pure oratory which I had never witnessed. It happened to be an introduction of the governor to the people and specifically to Gana, with the major portion being devoted to the reciting of their lineages; but Fall's *griot* genius was such that he could have spun the occasion into a frenzy speaking nothing but nonsense syllables. He worked his magic over a space of five minutes, at the end of which his straining voice was all but lost in the tumult from the crowd. Shouts arose from all about the arena; and directly behind my right ear a woman delivered a shrill keening, breaking out of it screaming "Fall, *suma jukkir* [Fall, my husband]!" I was overwhelmed; the place was abuzz; and now the governor himself finally stood to speak.

Speaking in Wolof, the man delivered a dry, passionless discourse in which he praised Gana and the other speakers, cited the virtues and accomplishments of the Party, said that the government would be unable to provide any advance money, and said that the best way for the people to help themselves and their country was to join the Party and to work their fields. As he finished the drumming began again, and there was a final short set of dancing climaxed by the *griot* M'Baye Diouf performing wild farming motions with his *gop*, celebrating the people's intention to cultivate their fields for the Party.

And with that, the *réunion* was over. The important persons retired briefly to the rear of Gana's boutique for a meal and consultation. Then the guests climbed into their Land Rovers and roared out of the village to the drumming of the *griots*, headed for the village of N'Gueme Issa where they were already five hours late for their third *réunion* of the day.

Back at the house we could hear drums and shouting still going on across the village as we relaxed and held a post mortem. Seidu moaned at the monumental indignity of M'Baye Diouf's *gop* dance and gave hilarious imitations of various of the speakers' elaborate ways of saying nothing at all. Everyone agreed that *Le Gouverneur* himself had been *"backhul dara* [worthless]," but nobody was surprised; and the only ones who seemed particularly upset about it were Seidu and myself.

Bity later told me that certain Serrers were going to *"wouti garab* [look for medicine]" to deal with the governor that night—and that this was really much more efficacious than anything that anyone could have said at the réunion. I asked him if he really believed they could do anything, and he assured me that they had done this sort of thing before. He said that several years previously an official from Bambey had given the village a hard time, that certain people had done certain things against him as soon as he had left, and that he had been killed in an automobile accident on his way back to Bambey. He said that I should wait and see—that *Le Gouverneur* would not be in office much longer.

A week later we were sitting in front of the house in the early morning. N'Djamé Sene's truck had just sped off towards M'Bouloktane; Saliou Diouf was throwing stones at the birds ravaging his bean patch across the way; and from down at the Cooperative we could hear the voices of young Gana and others entering the early stages of the day's arguments.

Bity and Aliou came in at the gate; and after greeting us Bity asked with a smile if we had heard he news about the governor. We hadn't; and he proceeded to inform us that the man had been put in prison during the last few days, his official offense being the hoarding and sale of welfare rice and flour.

Sitting in the gathering heat I tried to make sense of the news. I heard the clatter of a *charrette* and looked up to see Bity's father, old Gana, driving past the gate at a fast clip on his way to the road to visit his second wife. High on the charette seat in his deep blue *grand bou-bou*, his one eye focused intently on the path ahead of him, he passed quickly from sight behind the fence; and as I turned to face Bity I wondered why I should have doubted this news. *Le Gouverneur* was in prison; it was as simple as that. The thin, passionless man would never again be in a position of power over the village, whatever the reasons for his imprisonment.

I asked who the new governor would be, but neither Bity nor Aliou knew nor, in fact, was interested.

"*Khamuma chi dara* [I know nothing about it]," said Aliou, "*Waya cou mu nek, du gowa fi nyo* [But whoever he is, he won't come out here in a hurry]. *Dema la co wackh, dugadugadug, du gowa fi nyo* [Let me tell you, he's not going to come out here in a hurry]."

Photographs

Bity Sene and Joe

Guedj Sene

Sey Dieng

Modou Diouf

Heat, Sand, and Friends

N'Djémi Faye

Amadou Badiane

Sohel N'Gom and Modiane M'Bao

Amadou Badiane in his manioc patch

Photographs

Going to the well

Séssene granaries

Semping—Malik Diouf and WalySene

Sey Tchiao and Sey Dieng

Chapter 4

Laobé

Laobé

"*Bal ma ak* [Forgive me]," said Badiane, bowing deferentially at the gate, clutching his prayer beads in one hand and a pair of manioc roots in the other.

"*Bal na la* [I forgive you]." I completed the exchange and rose to greet him, stepping out from under the shade roof into the blazing afternoon sun. Silently, he presented me with the manioc, and when I invited him to join us for tea he conveyed via gestures that he would sit with us for a while.

It was Korité, the celebration of the end of Ramadan, the Moslem month of fasting. Purged by a month of abnegation and contemplation, a good Moslem was to let no malicious words pass his lips; and the normally loquacious Badiane, taking no chances, was restricting himself to this ritual exchange—"*Bal ma ak—Bal na la.*" I had heard it several times today among the Wolof down in the center of the village. Our Serrer friends were not so pious, but they responded respectfully when Badiane addressed them in this manner.

He sat down on the porch, and I took the large brown roots into the house to add to the mounting pile of food which we had amassed now that the crops were ripening. They joined a couple of handfuls of Saliou Diouf's beans, a number of heads of millet from an old Serrer in M'Bomboye, a large bag of peanuts which had accumulated incrementally, and a gourd of *mouraké* (ground peanuts, millet and sugar) which Bity's mother had made for us. This last I brought back out with me and passed around to our friends in the yard.

The day was hot; and punctuating it at intervals, in seeming protest against the brutal heat, was the anguished, incredibly raucous cry of a donkey in heat, wandering around by the schoolrooms attended closely by four or five males. Bity was about to make tea, sitting on a mat on the sand under the shade roof.

With us this Korité afternoon were Waly Sene, M'Baye Tchiao, Aliou Diouf, N'Dik Sene, old Gana, and Modou N'Gom, plus a few children whom we had previously dispatched to the farthest corners of the village to purchase the ingredients for tea — Abdou Dieye to N'Djamé Sene's for tea and Medina biscuits, Baye Gaye to Tchiendou N'Diaye's for charcoal, Modou Tchiao to Yibou N'Diaye's for sugar. The ingredients were assembled now. The water was heating in a kettle on the little brazier that the *teugues* had made, and we all awaited the rare and consummate pleasure of tea in the shade on a hot afternoon.

Two evenings before, Radio Senegal had announced the appearance in Dakar of the first sliver of the new moon that signaled the end of Ramadan. Here in the village, however, the moon had been obscured by clouds. The strict Moslems of the village had continued their fast until seeing the moon with their own eyes the following night. For most everyone else, however, the confusion had resulted in two successive days of celebration.

Thus this was our second day of Korité; and although of those present only the silent Badiane had fasted, all were fully appreciating the extended respite from work in the fields. The government had finally dispersed a cash advance on the peanut money, enabling everyone to afford some rice and meat for the holiday or to finally purchase some new clothes.

The day was particularly hot, and the glaring sand in the unshaded portion of the yard intensified the pleasure of simply sitting in the shade and talking while the afternoon passed. *"Tog di wackhtan rek mo backh* [Just sitting and talking is good]," ran the oft-repeated phrase, a classic embodiment of the ideal of *djam a-rek.*

Ramadan had been very hard this year. The weather had been relentlessly hot, and the work in the fields had been heavy. Among the Serrers of Séssene whom we knew, none had kept up the fast for more than two days except for young Gana, who no longer cultivated a field. A number of Wolof down in the *dukaba* had fasted throughout, most of them likewise having no work in the fields. Our friend Seidu had valiantly lasted a week.

It had been in the late afternoon of the first day of Ramadan that Waly Sene had been sitting with us, just as he was now, after working all day in the sun without water, without *guru*, without even swallowing his own spit. That morning he had prepared for himself a gourd of bisap juice which was now waiting back in his compound for the moment when he heard Badiane singing the evening prayer down in N'Dondol Oulof. We had been sitting enjoying the gradual lessening of the day's heat when Badiane's high clear *"Allaaaah Akbaaaaaaar…"* had come wafting up informing us of day's end and catching Waly by surprise. He had leaped to his feet, sprinted across the way to Séssene and his own compound, and then collapsed in a dead faint as he reached his *neg*. That had been the extent of the fast for him.

He was not alone. The general opinion among most of our Serrer friends was that fasting a day or two at the beginning of the month and a day or two at the end was sufficient service to the custom to feel virtuous on Korité. While a number had carried out this compromise observance, however, most of them rejected the idea of the fast entirely. I had visited old Latendeo Sene, old Gana's brother and young Gana's father, this very morning and had asked him facetiously whether or not he had fasted.

With characteristic irreverence he had launched into an indignant tirade against the value of anything which advocated unnecessary discomforting of the body.

"I talked with Allah three nights ago," he had said to me, "and I told him: 'Allah: Go ahead take me if you want to—I'm ready—but I'm not going to comply with this foolishness!'"

Despite religious differences, however, everyone from Latendeo to Badiane observed and enjoyed Korité. It was an occasion of visiting and gift-giving, especially a particular custom whereby members of the lower castes—*griots, teugues,* and *laobés*—demanded and received gifts from just about everyone else. We had received gifts of food from various hands; and we were taking advantage of the imminence of our departure from the village by bestowing many of our extraneous possessions upon our friends in the form of gifts.

A few times during the two days, groups of *griot* children had found us at home and demanded *dewinels* [Korité gifts], and we had obliged them with trifles. Also, a couple of *teugue* women whom we knew had stopped by to demand their *dewinel*; but they did this often, Korité or no. They so delighted us with the inexhaustible energy and enthusiasm with which they invested their greetings that we could seldom begrudge them a gift. We would try to see how long we could maintain a fluent exchange of greetings with them before they would break off to ask for food.

Bity was almost ready to serve the first round of tea now. He had filled the *barada* with tea, washed it once with water which he discarded, then refilled it with boiling water and set it aside to steep alongside the waiting line of shot glasses. Then he had cracked apart the hard cone of sugar with the heel of one of the shot glasses and stuffed several chunks of it in with the tea, after which came a series of pourings into the glasses from a spectacular height and re-pourings into the barada to dissolve the sugar and cool the tea. Finally came the last tall pouring of the dark amber liquid, and the glasses were passed out by Modou N'Gom.

This first round was harsh and bitter, despite the amount of sugar employed. It was considered dangerous for pregnant women to drink it. Succeeding rounds, made from the same tea, would get progressively weaker until the tea was exhausted, with the second and third pouring being the finest.

I took the hot little glass between my thumb and forefinger and held it up to my nose. The smell was sharp and strong; and the heat rising from it drew a patch of sweat out onto my forehead. I took a loud tentative sip, sucking in enough air with the hot liquid to cool it. It was acrid and strong, thickened somewhat by the sugar. It was hot. I sucked down the rest of the glass rather quickly and let the sweat break out all over my face. The effect was purgative, a sort of total immersion in heat, and in its wake, the mere external heat of the day washed almost pleasantly over me. Nobody spoke.

Modou collected the glasses while Bity launched into preparations for another round; and we all began to talk about the harvest. The crops had turned out to be marginal this year—the millet barely adequate, the peanuts poor. Much of the millet had been felled now, with the heads cut and stacked to dry and the stalks waiting to be collected and used in fencing and housing. Some of the peanut plants had been uprooted and piled up to dry, waiting for the peanuts to be beaten free of the plants themselves and then sorted out in the wind, with the dried detritus being given to the horses.

The past few weeks had been the time of *"suntés,"* when a man would call on friends and relations to come and work in his field on a particular day in order to overcome by communal energy the final amounts of work which had accumulated. Nearly each day someone in Séssene had held a *sunté*, until if seemed as if the fields were actually being worked collectively. Members of a man's matrilineage, to which his field ultimately belonged, would be called to his *sunté* along with men who were simply his friends in the village.

Bity had held a *sunté* recently for one of his fields of millet, calling a group of relatives from near M'Bah Faye whom I had never met or seen before in the village. Waly had hosted one a few days before that in his biggest field of peanuts. He had about the best peanuts of anyone I knew; and he needed them, for at 25 years of age and unmarried he was beginning to try to amass money for a bride price.

Bity's peanuts were few and small, as were his father's, M'Baye Thiao's, N'Dik's, and Aliou's. Each man would earn the equivalent of about $50 from them; but the millet, at least, was adequate. Before long it would be time to put it into the granaries, calling for an all-day affair called a *"semp"* which was occasion for great celebration and song. Four or five men would stand inside of a grainery while others outside loaded it with the heads of millet; and they would chop away with their *gops* at the millet beneath them, singing semping songs as they slowly rose to the top of the grainery over the course of the day. Their chopping left the grains intact but pulverized the stalk from which they had been separated; and the mixture would eventually be sorted in the wind by the women prior to the long process of pounding and sifting involved in making the evening meal. The chickens would get the *tchiokh* [chaff], or it would be traded to itinerant Naars for salt.

Modou Diouf passed by the gate now and waved, shouting a greeting which we all returned. He was forced to hold one arm over his head because of a bad sore on his armpit; and he was headed out to his field despite the holiday. As he disappeared we exclaimed among ourselves at his misfortune; and I heard once again the familiar laugh of helpless subjugation to the travails of life.

"*Ché waye,*" Aliou exclaimed with sadness, "*Da dokh chi chiorno rek*" [He's got it bad].

"*Reo-mi backhul reine*" [The country's no good this year], said M'Baye Tchiao shaking his head, "*Reo-mi backhatul dara dara dara*".

Badiane clucked a sound of disapproval at such talk and took his leave, nodding to everyone in turn and walking into the sun and out the gate in his jaunty, rolling stride.

Aliou began talking about a project which he had heard of wherein the government was paying men to settle with their families someplace in the eastern part of Senegal, trying to establish villages there for some reason. I had heard of such efforts and heard that they inevitably failed; that the transplants failed to take. Aliou was intrigued, however, and was listing all the benefits he had heard that one would receive.

"*Mandé man* [As for me]," said N'Dik from his hammock, "*Dina dem Amerique* [I'm going to America]. *Suma am-on pass, demai dem leygi, leygi rek* [If I had a ticket I'd go right now]," and he made the motion of an airplane taking off.

"*Mandali*" exclaimed Bity, laughing as he poured the second round of tea from a dramatic height, "*Wackhtan-bi niekhul* [This discussion is unpleasant]. *Degil N'Dik,* if you go there you'll be lonely — and they don't have tea over there." He was protecting us from the tedium of incessant talk about America, and I didn't bother to contradict him.

Modou passed out the shot glasses again, their amber content slightly lighter now. Conversation stopped and was replaced by another chorus of airy sipping. Its bitterness softened now, the tea was hot, strong and sweet. Once again it intensified both the heat of the day and the relief of the shade.

We sat in silence and then Waly exclaimed from his hammock. A little hedgehog was lolling in the cool sand beneath him, breathing in tiny, rapid little pants, having been driven from his home in the horse's hay beside us by the extreme heat. Aliou poked it and it curled into a prickly ball; but before long it resumed its dust bath.

Aliou resumed his talk of the new villages, but Gana cut him off, saying *"Wackhtan bo-bou niekhul; amul ndjerine* [That talk is unpleasant; it's useless]"; and Aliou demurred. Despite his own periodic travels Gana was upset by the urges of the younger generation to leave the village, as the pull of their roots seemed to be losing the inviolable strength it once had had.

Aliou himself was something of an example of the problem. Some years before, he had gone to Dakar and stayed for a number of years, working on the docks, until it appeared that he had left the village for good. Bity said that he had even learned to speak fluent French, a skill he no longer possessed. His father had finally visited him in the city and found him living in the household of a rich Peuhl, at the man's beck and call. Bity had described Aliou's father horrified description of the Peuhl sitting eating rice and calling loudly for Aliou to come and play his *ridi* for him, which he dutifully did. The father, appalled at his son's ignominious existence, had appealed to him to return to the village; but he had refused. The man had then enlisted the aid of old Gana and others; and they had worked magic charms on Aliou whose power was such that he had returned to the village never again to leave.

The same had once been done to Modou Yatte, a man considerably older than Aliou who lived across the way. The women of his compound had despaired of his wanderlust, which continually left them ill provided for, and they had finally resorted to the same solution as Aliou's father. *"Suma baye backhul le* [my father's bad]," Bity had laughed with a mixture of pride, disapproval and awe when he described the plight of poor homebound Modou Yatte: *"Cocou munatul dem fen* [That one can't go anywhere anymore]."

In both cases the magic had been worked as an extreme last resort at the desperate solicitation of their own kin. It was not a casual sort of intervention. I knew that Gana was now somewhat worried about his middle son N'Diar. At the beginning of the rainy season N'Diar had expressed his intention to go to a village near Kaolak to work a field in the household of some rich man there, because he thought the chances were better for a successful crop there. Gana had disapproved, wanting N'Diar to stay home and contribute to the work effort of the compound; but N'Diar had gone anyway, sneaking off with his wife and child in their charrette in the dead of night.

A familiar voice was approaching the gate, now, singing as it came:

"*Dotuma ré geyndi eh yellio* [I will no longer kill the lion...]. *Dotuma ré geyndi eh yellioooOOOoooOOOooo...*".

It was Baddu Sene, singing a semping song which I had recorded the previous year at N'Diar's *semp*, and singing it complete with a perfect imitation of the wavering of the sound on my tape recorder as the batteries ran down. We laughed at this new manifestation of his oral genius and watched as he came in the gate.

"*Ché way, Fall, ana magnetophone-ba? Nan co indi* [Come on, Fall, where's the tape recorder? Why don't you bring it out]. *Way-um niekhne chi man torop, way* [I love the sound it makes]."

"*Ndeysan, da panne* [Oh dear, it's broken]," I said to him; and he glowered at me, knowing that I just didn't want to wear out my precious batteries.

"*Ché way, bull ma meré way. Get na co deg, way* [Don't make me mad; I haven't heard it in a long time]."

Baddu was 14 years old. He spoke three languages beautifully and could mimic any sound with humor and precision. I looked into his eyes: they were his mother Kodu's, dark and brooding. Behind them smoldered a fire which in an instant could light up with pleasure or flash with ill will. He was always trying to get me to go somewhere or to do something; and I was always disappointing him. And since we liked each other, and he was always around, I was often the focus for his moods, fending off his dark eyes or bathing in the warmth of his good humor.

"*Cheh way, Fall,*" he said now with a mixture of the two, "*Nan co indi, way.*"

"*Eh, Laobé,*" said Waly from his hammock, "*Bay-il wackh bo-bou* [Drop that talk]."

Baddu's eyes flashed. "*Bull ma co wackhati, Waly* [Don't say that to me again]," he returned.

"*Nopil yo, way, no-il rek* [Be quiet, you; just be quiet]," said Waly, his anger rising.

"*Way yo Waly, dema co booga deg rek* [Come on, Waly, I just want to hear it]. *Dema booga deg mu né 'Eh, yellioooOOOoooOOOoooo.*'"

We all laughed, and the mood was repaired as quickly as it had decayed. Bity passed the third round of tea. I gave my glass to Baddu, as he hadn't had any yet. He refused; I insisted. He took it and was happy again.

Baddu was *laobé*, as Waly had addressed him. Laobés were woodworkers, and thus holders of the lower social standing accorded to members of artisan castes. In addition to the distinctions of their particular skill and their particular social standing, they also shared a heritage that was distinct from either the Wolof or the Serer among whom they lived:

They had their own language, which was related to Peuhl and Toucouleur. Laobé.

Baddu's family lived in a single compound on the edge of Séssene, next to the Sene compounds; and they spoke Serrer in addition to laobé and Wolof. The only other laobés with whom I was acquainted were affiliated with the Wolof portion of the village and lived over in a little hollow of land called N'Djomar near the haunted well Djamsila.

Laobé was as incontrovertible a fact of Baddu's being as was his physical appearance. When Waly called him "Laobé" he was calling up and affirming all the nuances of the relationship between laobés and Serrer farmers in the overall social order—one that contained a mixture of respect for the woodworkers' skill, disdain for their social standing, and the very real friendship which lay between them. Waly's calling Baddu "Laobé" had the quality of a friendly cuff, but the reminder of the lesser status of laobés still chafed. It chafed; and this was visible in Baddu's dark eyes and his moods. Black moods were his birthright.

"*Modou N'Gom, munolo saga* [Modou N'Gom, you don't know how to curse]," I had heard him say to Modou one day with disdain; and it was true. In contrast to Baddu, Modou was perpetually bright and happy; and even though he could be hurt, and sad, and confused, he hadn't Baddu's smoldering fire within him. Baddu could saga, on the other hand. He could saga as well as any 14 year old anywhere on earth. He had both an extraordinary verbal facility and the source from which both curse and insult sprang—that stew of feelings resultant from the perpetual hand against the shoulder, the perpetual cuff of social placement.

Baddu could saga; but along with the shadow of resentment which flickered across his face, was a resolute pride in that which was uniquely laobé—the deep warmth of his family compound, the refuge of his own language, the pride in the woodworker's skill. Baddu was filled with love for these things.

The bench on which Nini was sitting as she sipped her tea had been given her by Baddu. One day he had announced that he was going to make it for her. He took his father's ax out to where a big branch of a *cad* tree had fallen a couple of weeks earlier and patiently chopped off a section about a foot and a half long. This he carried back to the shade of the gigis tree next to his compound in Sessene where the members of this family often sat during the day carrying out various chores. He set directly to work with his grandfather's *saota* (a small one-handed adze), chiseling away for two days as the bench gradually emerged and presenting it to Nina when it was done. It was a beautiful bench. It was the gift of a laobé.

Saliou Diouf now paused at the gate on his way down to the center of the village and came in when he saw that we were home. Tall, handsome, pleasant in manner, he was a well-respected man in the village—a hard-working Serrer farmer and *borom keur* [head of household].

He was wearing a new *bou-bou*, which I admired after we had greeted one another. This meant, I knew, that he now possessed two good bou-bous in addition to the tattered one that he wore each day to his fields. It was a source of both pride and relief for a man like Saliou to own two good bou-bous: He would not have to spend any money on clothes for a long time to come. He fingered the material as if somewhat perplexed by such luxury and agreed that it was a fine garment. He wore it well.

"The women at my house are very happy because of you," he said: *"Lolou backhne* [that is good]." I had visited his compound earlier in the day carrying a bag containing six old cut-off nightgowns of Nini's which I intended to bestow upon Saliou's wife Gaye, old Moussane Diouf in the next compound, and certain other women up in the complex of compounds known as N'Dioufene. Saliou had not been at home, but Gaye, his mother, and another woman had been there. When one of then had half-jokingly demanded a *dewinel* I had produced three of the tops with a flourish and suddenly found myself the focus of their delighted celebration. They shouted, sang and danced in front of me; and the commotion quickly attracted two more women from the adjoining compound, who also received tops and added to the carrying-on. I beat a hasty retreat lest the women outnumber the gifts and gave the last one to Moussane Diouf next door in the privacy of her own *neg* [hut].

"*Lolou backhne,*" Saliou repeated seriously, as if I were finally getting the hang of his culture. While we chatted I took a mental inventory of the people in the yard and determined that I had already given a present to each of them except Saliou; and I presented him with a small five-liter jerry can, which he had admired long ago. He was very pleased. He explained in his seemingly jocular manner which one knew from his eyes to be serious that he would use it to carry water with him to his fields and that it was doubly valuable because every time he used it, it would remind him of me. I fought back the old worry about being flattered and conned and let myself enjoy his genuine pleasure. It was a warm moment.

Before he left to continue on his way, he took me out of earshot behind the house and asked me in serious tones to be sure to stop by his compound later on in the afternoon. He would be returning home very shortly, he said, and had something he wanted to give me. We returned to the front and he passed out the gate and continued on his way, new bou-bou on his back and jerry can in his hand.

Bity was pouring the fourth round of tea. It was light in color, now, but as hot as ever. The hard edge of the tea was dominated by the undiminished sugar. About us, the heat of the day had now faded slightly with the tea. Only one more round after this would be worthwhile.

Old Gana rose and took his leave, having some business to attend to elsewhere. M'Baye Tchiao laughed as he left, saying that the old man was already lining up the accumulation of enough *n'goyne* [peanut straw] to feed his horse through the coming year. He had lived through too many years in this village to get caught short-handed during the dry season.

Bity sent Modou N'Gom out to get some dried peanut plants from Gib Tchiao's field and make *pitine*. Soon the boy reappeared outside the gate with an armful of the plants, piled them in the sand, and set then afire. As the dry debris burned quickly away he foraged for the peanuts, loaded them in his shirtfront, and brought them in to us. With the shells scorched black, the nuts themselves were roasted hot and delicious. It was the best of all possible ways of eating peanuts; and of course it was only possible this once a year, at harvest time.

I told Baddu that it would not be long before he would hear the semping songs for real, that that was better than any tape recording. He agreed reluctantly, still longing for the magic of the tape. Bity began preparing the final round of tea, and the afternoon continued to slide effortlessly by.

Later on, after the fifth glass of tea, I took leave of our guests and headed up to Saliou Diouf's to fulfill my promise to visit. The world beyond the gate had already reached its ripeness and was beginning to dry out now, headed towards its ultimate grey/brown. My millet was down, the stalks stacked haphazardly about the field. The gourds bulging on the vines which Bity's mother had planted were beginning to pull down our fence. The panorama of the countryside had been opened up once again. Once again I could see as far as the trees would allow towards M'Bomboye to the north. Grass and bushes now covered much of the land, and would cover it until they were either cut down for hay, roofing, granaries or whatever, or simply cleared away for next year's planting.

Down the path I saw some goats trying to nudge their way through the thorny border of Saliou's bean patch, and I detoured to shoo them away. Behind me, the beleaguered donkey in heat let loose another series of soul-rending brays. Ahead of me along the path most of the millet had been cut down, except for a small stand of the late-ripening *basi*, which bobbed its graceful heads gently to the slight movement of the air around it.

As I reached Saliou's compound I looked back at our own house and remembered what a mystery the physical layout of the village had seemed when we had first arrived, with the millet up over our heads before harvest. More than once while making our introductory rounds of social visiting we had gotten lost this short distance from home. Once we had visited Saliou's compound twice within ten minutes, not realizing until we were well into our greetings that we had delivered the same spiel of broken Wolof to the same people a few minutes earlier.

I entered the compound now, and after a warm flurry of greetings with the women I found Saliou puttering around in a little back yard, which was accessible only through his own *neg*. He ushered me back inside and we sat down—he on the bed and I on a wooden chest.

The space inside, about ten feet square, was cool and dark, a relief from the glare of the compound. I took off my sandals to dig into the sand with my toes. Beside the bed were two flat rocks about the size of bricks on which to rest one's feet as one sat on the bed and washed them free of sand before sleeping. There was a round clay *ndah* in the corner by the entrance, and Saliou dug in a patch of wet sand beside it to produce a guru, well preserved, which he washed and shared with me.

As I savored its bitterness and my eyes became accustomed to the light I looked at the underside of the roof, which rose to a peak at the center. Stuck here and there between the frame and the grass of the roof were a good many of Saliou's possessions — heads of millet to be used for seed, a knife, a couple of gri-gri belts, various little packets of brown paper, a coil of a baobab rope, and so forth.

There too were his notebook and pen from Nini's French class. I remembered Saliou getting up constantly in the middle of class to check on his bean patch, and the skeptical look on his face as he regarded letters that he had written with his own hand. I remembered the gradual realization that neither he nor anyone else in the class was every really going to learn French and the mutual feeling that despite this the class was a thing of pride and value. I remembered sitting here on this same chest in Saliou's neg and watching him and his nine year old son, Moustapha, who attended the village school, arguing affectionately over Moustapha's slate about the correct way of spelling "Saliou", with both of them being wrong.

"Fall," Saliou addressed me now, "they tell me that you're going to be put in the army when you return to your country. You should have told me. There are things that can be done about it."

I said that it was true, but that I was receiving aid from various people in the village, as well as a certain old Serrer on the road to M'Bah Faye and the marabout in M'Bouloktane.

"Never mind that," he said. "I'm going to give you something now that will protect you as long as you keep it with you. This is not a trifling matter; this is something that will protect you always."

I said that I understood and that I was very honored by his concern. I was surprised, actually. I had had no idea that Saliou had any abilities of this sort. Certain people had established public reputations, and their aid could be solicited by anyone for a price. Others had more guarded reputations, and their aid could not be bought. Bity had told me that many of the most powerful possessors of this sort of *kham-kham* [knowledge] were the least accessible—that men like his father never sold their services because that tended to place them at everyone's disposal. Saliou was about forty years old, a respectable Serrer farmer and head of household but not a man with this sort of reputation. I had never heard his name connected with *garab* before; but there was no question that he was serious about what he was saying.

He got down on his knees now and hunted around in the sand underneath his bed, finally withdrawing three gnarled pieces of wood, which I decided must be sections of tree root. Sitting back on the bed he took his knife from the ceiling and began to carve off a piece from the first one, saying that he would give me three different pieces which must always be kept together. We fell silent as he carved carefully away.

Suddenly, Saliou looked up as we heard a man's voice greeting the women outside in the compound. It was Gibril Gadjiaga, a man of Saliou's age, a laobé, who lived across the village in the place called N'Djomar and was undoubtedly making his scavenger's rounds in search of dewinels. Saliou quickly hid the pieces of wood and the knife under the bed and sat back upright as if we were merely talking.

"Laobé," he said to me in way of explanation, gesturing with his head towards the sound of Gibril's voice. I was annoyed by the intrusion, not only because he was interrupting this important matter between Saliou and me, but also because I rather disliked the man. I sensed that Saliou felt the same way, and I hoped that the laobé would not take up too much of our time.

He came to the door, peered in from the glare and entered, greeting us and sitting on the bed where Saliou gestured for him to sit. The two men began to talk while I remained quiet. They were contemporaries and were of rather similar status in the village despite the caste difference — Gibril a wily Wolof and Saliou a stolid Serrer. They talked small talk about crops and weather and family; and I had the impression that Saliou, like me, was waiting out the laobé's visit with his mind somewhere else.

After a while Gibril lounged back on his elbows, looked at Saliou with a self-satisfied smile, and asked, *"Ana suma dewinel* [Where's my Korité present]?", giving a palms-up 'where is it?' gesture with his hands. I glowered at him; but he and Saliou bantered easily back and forth, with Saliou fending him off and Gibril continuing to wheedle. Then, quite abruptly, Saliou leaned forward, reached across in front of Gibril, took his second good bou-bou from where it was hanging from the roof, and handed it to the man.

I was taken aback, and so, it seemed, was Gibril. He protested; but Saliou insisted, saying that he himself had the new one that he was wearing. Finally Gibril acquiesced, obviously very touched. His face glowed with good will, and my resentment of him began to melt.

"Diouf," he said earnestly, "this is a wonderful, wonderful thing. When I wear this I will always remember that my friend Saliou Diouf gave it to me; and thus it will always be much more than just a bou-bou. You are very good to give this to me." He then rose with the bou-bou over his arm, bathed us both in good feeling as he said his salutations, and left.

As we listened to him bidding goodbye to the women, Saliou recovered his roots and knife from under the bed and poised to set to work once again. He looked at me, seemed to feel some need for explanation, and gestured with his head towards the departed presence of the laobé.

"*Suma harit le* [He is my friend]," he commented simply, and resumed his carving.

Chapter 5

Adjuma

Adjuma

"Naar! Naar!"

The familiar voice—like its owner, thin, a trifle comical, but strong —sought me out from beyond the gate: "Naar!"

"No Naars around here that I know of," I called back and continued whatever I was doing.

"Naar! Naar!" It persisted.

"Nobody here by that name," I answered.

Naars were people of Arab blood who came down from Mauretania to run little hole-in-the-wall shops throughout Senegal; and although they were universally scorned, they managed to end up with most of the small change in the country tucked away in the folds of their dusty robes. Their lonely outposts could be found in every town above a certain size. The smallest Wolof child would walk into a Naar shop and yell, *"Naar! Kai jai ma way!* [Naar! Come here and sell to me!]," and the Naar would come and sell to him, ignoring the abuse and winding up with the money.

"Naar! Naar!" continued the man at the gate.

His name was Adjuma [Friday, mosque day], and he knew that I was not a Naar. He also knew that I knew he knew that I was not a Naar; but this was one of several alternative openings to our daily ritual. We would move on to the next movement after one or the other of us had conceded this portion of it.

"No Naars around here!" I maintained.

There was silence for a moment; and then from the gate came a plaintive, crooning "Bonjouououououour."

"Bonjour, Monsieur," I responded instantly, entering into the beloved second movement, which consisted of a parody of social greetings, in French, performed with accelerating energy and adamant pronunciation until our vocabulary of nonsense phrases failed us.

"Bonjour, Monsieur."

"Bonjour, Monsieur."

"Ca va ta bien."

"Ca va ma bien."

"Ca va ta blah."

"Ca va blah ca."

"Est-ce que ca ta blah?"

"M'Est-ce que va ma ca!"

"Ca va le cous-cous?"

"Ca va le tcheb-u-djen!"

"Ca va les arrachides?"

"Ca va le sauce de tomate arrigoni!"

I moved to greet him as he came through the gate in the herky-jerky gait which he used to convey an impression of speed. I extended my hand and he offered me his wrist, implying that he had been working so hard that his hand was all dirty and sweaty. I knew that he hadn't been working at all, and he knew I knew that he hadn't been working at all. I looked into his eyes and he gave me an intimate conspiratorial smile as he searched his mind for another line of bluff. He was a tall, thin, rather handsome man, with an infectious smile which bared extraordinary molar-like front teeth. He had been crazy for forty years.

"Ah, ma né [I say]," he said, peering at me craftily: *"Ma ne: Naar!"* he tried the name again in a voice which seemed to burst spastically from his mouth of its own accord.

"Adjuma, you know I'm not a Naar."

"*Wackh nga dug, wackh nga dug* [That's true]," he acknowledged without argument, as if I had spoken something very wise with which he was in complete agreement. "*Ah — ana wa Djourbel* [How's everyone in Djourbel]?"

"I've told you twenty times that I come from the other direction, across the ocean."

"*Kham-on na co* [I knew that]. *Ana wa Rufisque* [How's everyone in Rufisque]?"

"Farther than Rufisque!"

"Dakar, khana?"

"Adjuma," I spoke with a tone of mild admonishment.

He looked at me as if he knew I was putting him on even though he couldn't prove it. He grinned charmingly, and then asked abruptly, all joking aside now, "*Dow ma may nyari bunt u allumettes* [Won't you give me two sticks of matches]?" This, at last, was the end game of the whole exchange.

"*Nyari bunt u allumettes!*" I exclaimed with mock surprise. He grinned sheepishly, but stuck to his point.

"*Wow, wow. May ma nyari bunt u allumettes* [Yeah, yeah. Give me two sticks of matches]. *Am na pone té* [I have tobacco today]."

I produced the matches with a flourish: "*Am.*"

"*Wow kai, Wow kai* [Yes, indeed]," he muttered with no trace of emotion as his hand grasped what he had come for and he sat down on the corner of the porch to tend to his pipe.

During our time in the village Adjuma had become a regular visitor at our house. A bond had grown between us based partly on the mutual understanding, as we looked into each other's eyes, that we were both outside of the mainstream of village life — I because of my foreignness and he because of his craziness. I had grown to love the daily ritual that had evolved around what never ceased to be the heart of the matter and the essence of our relationship—his two sticks of matches. We would flirt with something deeper between us, and we would feign something less; but we both knew that the issue would eventually come down to *nyari bunt u allumettes*.

He accepted our presence in his universe with sublime indifference, as if we were the most temporal and unremarkable of phenomena. Nothing we said to him ever shook his calm or ruffled his dignity. He would respond to our efforts at conversation with a grave concurrence which implied a fundamental disbelief in the value of verbal communication above the level of necessity; and he would issue his own pronouncements with the same hollow gravity, as if he didn't ultimately care about what he was saying nor expect to be believed.

We existed in two separate worlds—I, a visitor on the merest periphery of the enveloping web of the village, and he so deeply enmeshed in that web that he seemed closer to the landscape and the trees than to the society of humans. And yet our spiritual paths did cross.

At moments during our daily charade his madness would seem to desert him as a refuge, and we would look very deeply into each other's eyes. It seemed at these moments that we understood that we had both everything in common and virtually nothing in common; and the business of the matches—entirely trivial but never forgotten—came to symbolize both. For a moment it would seem that we saw each other so clearly that there was nothing left to be said; and he would dispel and seal the moment by laying claim to his *nyari bunt u allumettes*.

He would sit for hours on the corner of the porch or in the sand by the fence, fiddling with his pipe while we had tea with friends or otherwise went about our business. We became used to having our conversation punctuated by gurgling from his direction as he blew saliva through his pipe stem, or by furious whispering and cursing as he argued with his voices.

"What's that you say, Adjuma?" someone would call over to him.

"I wasn't talking to you," he would respond with annoyance, or more often than not ignore them completely.

Our first encounter with him, shortly after we had arrived in the village, had been both mystifying and unsettling. He appeared in our yard in the dead of the night, speaking what was pure gibberish to our ears. After a long sequence of abortive efforts at communication on both our parts, during which he seemed both angry and offended, he walked slowly about the yard and sprinkled the trunks of the trees with water from the old tomato can which he carried.

Apparently, we found out later, this was his obsession, a service which he was compelled to perform by his voices. "Allah help you," Seidu told us, "if you ever cut down a tree in that old fool's presence."

At the time, we were bewildered; but we thanked him and felt relieved. Then, as he left, he revealed a glimpse of what we later came to know as the essential Adjuma: A resolute attempt at gravitas undercut by utter foolishness. He strode slowly out of the yard, his carriage erect and sober, trailing from his foot a long vine which had caught on his sandal, of which he was obviously aware but which through some confused sense of dignity he declined to acknowledge.

Soon it became a familiar sight to see Adjuma, tall and straight in his dusty, ragged old bou-bou, a rag on his head, his staff in one hand and tomato can in the other, trudging through the sand under the burning sun. And once he understood that he entertained us and touched us, our house became one of his daily refuges. His family was not quite so patient with him.

He lived in the compound where we ate every night—that of his brother, old Gana. He was fed and cared for there, his foolishness and lack of contribution to the work effort tolerated. M'Baye Tchiao, Gana's *djourbat*, had responsibility for maintaining his *neg* [hut], and M'Baye's wife Sey Dieng fed him. They regarded him as one might a sometimes amusing but generally burdensome animal.

"He's worse than a horse," M'Baye Tchiao said one night when I commented on how decrepit Adjuma's neg had become: "He digs inside of it and undermines it." He made frantic, rodent-like digging motions with his hands.

Indeed the next evening as we entered the compound we noticed that Adjuma's neg had been reduced to an utter hovel, having collapsed on top of him the previous night. M'Baye Tchiao rebuilt it; and Adjuma, insisting that there was a dead man buried there, proceeded to undermine it again. The next time he rebuilt it, M'Baye Tchiao buried thorns in the sand around the posts, so that Adjuma couldn't dig there. Stymied, Adjuma refused to sleep in it, insisting now that it should be moved a few feet in one direction; and after Gana had helped to dissuade him from sleeping at our house, which he claimed that he owned, he spent his nights beside his empty neg. When it rained he crawled under an old, collapsed section of fencing.

Old Gana had little tolerance left for his brother, and would berate him and even beat him when he felt shamed by his foolish behavior. Apparently Adjuma's forty years of exemption from the normal duties and responsibilities of being a man had worn his patience a little thin.

The two brothers had come of age during the time when the French were making the country their own through their technology and systems of organization. Stories of their father's time told of a world where the white man, while not unknown, was not yet in control of African destiny; but their own time had been marked by an increasing threat to the insular world of the village and the rural heritage of the Serrer.

Old Gana had been a strong chief. It was his pride that he had done full honor to the Serrer traditions and kept them alive and meaningful under the cultural friction before which they were now visibly eroding. Adjuma, on the other hand, had become a Catholic and had gone to learn from the white priests. There was a common understanding among his extended family that his *rabbs* [his family's devils] had made him crazy because of this desertion of tradition.

Although it had happened before he was born, Bity had told us the story of the actual time when Adjuma had gone crazy. Apparently he had been sitting against a tree over in Séssene studying his mission primer, and he had begun to read aloud from it:

"*Le singe monte l'arbre* [The monkey climbs the tree]."

And then he translated: "*Golo-gi yeg chi garab-gi.*"

"*Le singe monte l'arbre: Golo-gi yeg chi garab-gi. Le singe monte l'arbre: Golo-gi yeg chi garab-gi.*"

He repeated this several times, put the book down, and proceeded to laugh uncontrollably. It was the beginning of his craziness; and he had kept it up for forty years.

Bity said that his rabbs beat him, kicked him, and made him do things. We often saw him, sitting in the sand between our house and the schoolrooms, arguing angrily with the air about him, wincing as though he was being struck, and then getting up reluctantly and moving on, protesting vociferously all the while. Bity also said that Adjuma had said that his rabbs appeared to him as white men.

Apparently he had been quite violent in the early stages of his madness, bursting into compounds, claiming that he owned them and beating people; but time had calmed his violence, and he had eventually reached a peaceful symbiosis with the rest of life around him.

While we were living there a young man named Assane, who had been working in a factory in Dakar, had returned to the village in a similar state of madness. Strong and uncontrollable, he had terrorized the village sporadically for a couple of weeks, upsetting all the cauldrons of rice at a funeral, breaking into Guedj Sene's neg and ripping down all his *gri-gris* [magic charms], threatening his brothers with a knife, and so forth. The only physical sanction which had been brought to bear had come when several men from his own and neighboring compounds had tackled him to wash him with some special medicine that his family had purchased. Otherwise it was simply hoped that the madness would run its course, that the violence would work itself out. Like Adjuma, Assane was possessed by rabbs who beat him and ordered him about; like Adjuma they had possessed him as he was making a step between two worlds; and like Adjuma his rabbs appeared to him as white men. It remained to be seen whether his fury was a brief episode from which he would reemerge to assume a normal role in village life or whether, as had been the case with Adjuma, it was the beginning of a lifetime as a village *dof* [crazy person]. Every village had one.

    Bedeviled as he was, Adjuma managed, after his fashion, to maintain a certain dignity in his daily existence. *"Dem-na suma tol té* [I went to my field today]," he would say in a confidential, manly boast: *"Son na lol"* [I'm really tired]!" He did in fact have a field, which Bity and M'Baye Tchiao had planted and which was nothing but a patch of grass and weeds after a few rains. He would often pass our gate in his solemn trudge with a bundle of millet on his head, which he had pilfered from other people's fields. He would take it down to the Wolof part of the village to Yibou N'Diaye's boutique, where he would trade it for tobacco; and then he would make his way back to our house for his *nyari bunt u allumettes*. And then he would sit and smoke. When times were bad he would smoke dried horse manure.

At the time of the peanut harvest he quietly launched into a new pattern of activity. He would sit in the sand at the Cooperative and beg handfuls of peanuts from farmers bringing their sacks to be weighed; and at the end of the day he would march solemnly back to the compound with the peanuts tied up in a scrap of cloth on his head and deposit them in a modest granary which he had woven for himself out of millet stalks.

"He says that he's going to cash them in at the Cooperative and then buy himself a new bou-bou," M'Baye Tchiao said. "I keep telling him to watch out, that someone is going to steal them. He sleeps next to them at night."

We all laughed and kidded Adjuma about his peanuts and his greed. He endured the derision with stoic dignity and went about his chosen task with single-minded purpose. Slowly, over the course of several weeks, his granary filled with peanuts.

Then one night as we entered the compound for dinner we noticed his granary collapsed and empty beside his hovel, and Adjuma was not there.

"Where's Adjuma?" we asked in astonishment.

"He's gone," M'Baye Tchiao said. "He's gone *chi alaba* [out in the bush]."

Apparently Adjuma had borrowed a burlap sack, hauled his peanuts down to the Cooperative on Modou Diouf's donkey, cashed them in, and then set off into the countryside with the money, saying that he couldn't buy a bou-bou in our village because people would cheat him there. Nobody knew where he had headed, but nobody seemed particularly concerned.

For three days, he was gone. We asked repeatedly about him, but everyone shrugged and assured us that he would be all right—that wherever he was he would be welcomed for the night, and that sooner or later he would return.

Then, the fourth night, as we crouched in the sand eating our dinner, in strode Adjuma wearing a brand new bou-bou, saying nothing to anyone as he passed regally through the compound and disappeared around the corner to his neg. Sey Dieng took him a bowl of *tcheré*.

Leaving after dinner, we passed his hut, and there he was, reclining like a king against his collapsed granary, one hand behind his head and the other holding the unlit pipe in his mouth. We greeted him and commented on his new bou-bou, but he didn't say a word, dismissing us with a solemn, benedictory wave of his pipe hand.

As we started out the compound door, however, he seemed suddenly to panic and called out to us.

"Ma né! Naar!" he called; and as I turned and met his eyes he capitulated and used my real name.

"Ma né — Fall," he said now with a hint of a smile, holding out his unlit pipe in explanation, *"Ma né — dow ma may nyari bunt u allumettes?"*

Chapter 6

Boré

Boré

The drums had been calling all day, pausing now and then while the griot children rested, but otherwise tugging persistently at the back of everyone's mind. This was it: The climax of the wrestling season; the match of the year; the resolution of arguments which had been brewing in the village for weeks; the showdown between the two giants of the arena—Halifa, the incomparable Halifa, and Boy Serrer *numero deux*.

The season had been building over the course of about two months. At the beginning of the dry season—after the peanuts had been sold, with money in the village and no work in the fields—the group of men who had organized matches in previous years met once again and decided, amidst great argument and debate, to continue the tradition.

Saliou Diouf headed the group; and Yibou N'Diaye kept accounts in Arabic. Primer money was contributed by all the members, including ourselves; a suitable open area between Séssene and N'Dondol Oulof was ringed off with millet stalk fencing; and word was dispersed throughout the countryside that on a particular day the first match of the season would take place. Now, with matches having been held each week, the season had reached its climax. There remained only one pairing which could generate interest, and it was the grandest of them all: Halifa versus Boy Serrer II.

The season had been even more exciting than people had said it would be. It was the pride of the village, the best in all the countryside.

I had not expected this because the village was unable to host a particularly vibrant market day on its weekly turn in the region; but apparently the principles and traditions governing the market system were different from those at work with the wrestling matches. Our village had succeeded in being a cultural magnet if not a commercial one.

This afternoon, with the drums calling but a couple of hours left before the occasion itself, I was on my way over to visit Latendeo Sene, brother of old Gana and father of young Gana and Guedj. The blustery old man had berated me every time I had seen him in the past two weeks for not visiting him. *"Lou té nga nyo suma keur* [Why don't you come to my compound]?," he would ask in accusation, *"Ah! Bay nga ma leygi* [You've deserted me now]!" So I was going to perform this social courtesy now, when the approaching wrestling match would provide a natural horizon to Latendeo's long-windedness.

The approximate center of Séssene was a large open space surrounded by compounds and shaded by a huge *bentenyi* tree. Now, during the dry season, there were always one or two groups of men sitting together in the sand here, in addition to those under the laobés' *gigis* tree and the Diouf tree up the way, passing the day talking and playing a variety of games in the sand. The game currently in season — apart from dammes, which was played with wooden pieces on a board and thus transcended seasons — was *yoté*, in which the players used a particular twist of seed casing from a tree which had just dropped them on the ground and stems from *dharkasay* fruits which had also recently ripened. When these pieces passed out of season so would the game itself.

On hot evenings most of these men would be out here again, lying on mats and talking under the stars as the earth cooled beneath them and the women and children slept inside the compounds. It was a time when the ideal of *djam a-rek* [peace only] seemed perfectly realized. Occasionally

I would join them for an hour these evenings, and we would talk about their world or about my own country, or perhaps Aliou Diouf could be coaxed into playing his ridi; but most often Nini and I simply heard their voices as part of the surrounding night as we lay in our hammocks with our own sense of peace settling down upon us.

Here in mid-afternoon, with the drums slowly beginning to build, all talk was about the upcoming fight. Two men were sitting facing each other playing dammes, but the crowd which ordinarily would have surrounded them—exhorting, advising and attempting to make their moves for them if they hesitated too long—sat apart from them now, discussing Halifa and Boy Serrer. Guedj was there, and both Waly Senes, both N'Dik Senes, Malik Diouf, N'Gagne Tchiao, young Adjuma, and several others, and I paused for a moment to chat.

Adjuma had just returned from Bambey where he spent most of his time these days hoping to get a job driving a bush taxi (he possessed a Senegalese driver's license). He said that people in the town were talking about the match and that several of the fonctionaires were planning to come out to see it. Waly, who had spent the previous year in Dakar, was trying to one-up the rest by talking about matches he had seen there; but they would have none of it. N'Dik N'Deo called to mind a match in the village two years before when one wrestler had had the whole side of his face bloodied by a blow from his opponent; and everyone laughed the embarrassed laugh which Bity had used when describing the years of drought and which seemed to be reserved for things discordant or unhealthy generally. Guedj reminded me of the bet which we had riding on the match and said he had heard that Halifa had been beaten recently at a town about twenty miles away. And so the conversation went.

With considerable effort, I had finally determined the origin of Boy Serrer's name. "Boy", it turned out, was indeed the English word "boy", but it carried none of the degrading connotations of the colonial usage. It was used instead as a term of affectionate respect, and thus the name Boy Serrer seemed to mean the same as the name "Kid Irish" might mean for an Irish boxer in America. Boy Serrer II was unquestionably the pride of the Serrers, with the Wolof Halifa being something of a villain. I maintained my support of Halifa in the face of my friends' loyalty to their own, however; and I took my leave, promising to see them at the match. They would all be there.

Under the laobés' tree Yib Sene, Baddu's uncle, was working on a gop handle, and another man whose name I didn't know was skinning a large monitor lizard which Yib had caught earlier and brought over to our house in a sack to frighten Nini. He had malaria and considered himself too weak to talk, conveying to me via gestures how good it was going to taste. Yib laughed, knowing that the idea was foreign to me. I greeted them as I passed and skirted the perimeter fence of old Gana's compound on my way to that of Latendeo, Guedj and young Gana.

Near the entrance to their compound Tchiachi Sene was working at the base of a baobab tree trying to secure one of the pendulous, velvety fruit which dangled from its stubby branches. He had bound together in series several millet stalks and lashed his knife to the very end; but due to the elastic bobbing of his tool and the awkward angle of the knife he was consistently unable to cut free the most voluptuous of the fruit at which he was aiming. I called encouragement; and he laughed and returned to this task with the seemingly endless patience I had seen so often in the village.

Entering the compound I greeted the women who were there—young Gana's mother N'Diaye, two of his wives, one of Guedj's wives, and two others whose names I did not know—and presented myself at Latendeo's door saying, *"Konk, konk,"* the Serrer oral equivalent of a knock. His wife Badiane emerged from the back, ushered me in; and before I could protest she proceeded to shake Latendeo, who was sound asleep on the bed.

It took a while before the old man understood what was going on, the room being dark, his eyes being bad, and his sleep having been deep; but we eventually arranged ourselves beside each other on the edge of his bed looking out to the back where his chickens were scratching in the sand.

"Ma né," he said abruptly after a moment of silence, *"Toubab dina am boré* [Does the white man ever have wrestling]?"

I answered with the usual "Yes, but it's not exactly the same," which provided all the opening he needed to launch into a line of proud bluster.

"I'll say it's not the same," he said. "The *boré* of the Serrer has no equal—it exists nowhere else. Nowhere else can you find it. My son Guedj went to France and fought with the toubabs everywhere; but they had no *boré* to match ours."

"There are good fighters in my country too."

"Toubabs don't know about real *boré*."

"There are black men too in my country—as strong as Halifa and Boy Serer."

"There are black men in America?"

"Sure, I've told you that before."

"With skin just like this of mine?"

"Sure."

"No there aren't."

"Yes, there are."

"If there are black men in your country they are black toubabs— they aren't my kin."

"Some of them may be your kin."

"Do they eat millet?"

"No."

"Then they're not my kin."

"Nobody knows."

Silence ensued, as he pondered this conundrum.

"Ma né, is the wrestling here pleasing to you?" he asked suddenly.

"I think it's fantastic."

"It's no good at all."

"What do you mean? You don't think Boy Serrer and Halifa are any good?"

"They're the best there is today, but they can't compare with what used to be."

"It used to be better than this afternoon's match?"

"No comparison. We used to boré so hard it would make your head hurt to watch."

"Did you ever boré?"

"Did I ever boré!"

"Yeah, did you ever boré?"

"Did I ever boré! Did your father ever undo his pants? In all the countryside there was no-one faster than I!"

"I didn't ask if you could run."

"I could run, and I could fight. There was nobody faster and nobody fiercer. Phew, I could hit. Do you see this fist here? In all the countryside from N'Goye to M'Bouloktane no-one could hit harder than I could."

"I hear you got hit pretty hard yourself once out in N'Diamane. Someone told me that you woke up and didn't know where you were."

"I don't know what you're talking about. I never wrestled in N'Diamane. Your mother and your father wrestled that day in N'Diamane."

"I heard it was you."

"No-one was fiercer than I, and no-one was faster. Ah, there was one night that I was sleeping in Gogui Yatte's father's neg in N'Diamane, and when we woke up in the morning we found that our things had been stolen during the night. We stormed and cursed. We found their tracks, grabbed our machetes and started to run while the earth was still cool.

"The footprints ran west, and we ran with the sun behind us. We passed here in the early morning and headed out toward N'Goye; we passed there and headed towards M'Bouloktane. We ran and ran until we were tired and then ran and ran some more. Everyone dropped behind me but I kept running. I ran and ran until I wanted to die. In the whole countryside there was no-one faster."

The old man stopped speaking and nodded to himself on the bed, losing himself in the memory.

"So, what happened?" I prompted.

"What happened! Why I ran and ran until I was tired; I ran until I wanted to die; I ran through the heat of the day. And then in the afternoon I came upon them, three of them, three Peuhls, sitting underneath a dakar tree with all our things. I was upon them before I knew it, and my companions were far, far behind.

"The three of them laughed at me, but I still had my machete. I shook it at them and shouted: 'Not one of you is man enough to fight me. I'll fight you all, but one at a time. Let he who wants to offer his nose for sale step forward and I'll cut it off for him.' That frightened them, and they all ran off, leaving our things under the dakar tree.

"They thought that I was finished with them, but I ran after them. I chased them all the way to M'Bouloktane and through the village and out the other side into the swampy ground of the *marigot*. When I finally stopped they were up to their waists in mud and howling like they wanted to die; and when I got back to the dakar tree my companions still hadn't caught up. I tell you I was tired that day: Dugadugadugadug, I was tired that day."

I commented on the story, and he repeated in his wavering voice, his eyes still closed, still living in the story: *"Son-on na lol, kirogue* [I was really tired that day]; *dugadugadug, son-on na lol."*

"Badiane!" he shouted suddenly, waking from his reverie, *"Indil sow* [Bring some curdled milk]!"

I had long since learned that it was more trouble than it was worth to try to decline an offer of food; and *sow* was one treat that I consumed with relish at every opportunity. Badiane brought in a medium-sized gourd with the curdled milk at the bottom and a smaller, hand-sized gourd floating in it. Then she handed me a can of water and a box of sugar cubes. Latendeo watched as I diluted the milk, added some sugar cubes, and began crushing and stirring them up with the hand gourd.

"Ma né," he said, *"Sow am-ne Amerique?"*

"Well yes, but it's not exactly the same."

"Toubabs have cows?"

"Sure. Out in the country they have lots of hem."

"Do the black men there have cows?"

"Some do, I guess, but not too many."

"When it's hot there do you drink sow?"

"Sometimes, but this sow here is better."

I tested it, added a bit more sugar, stirred it up, and then took several long swallows. It slid cool down my throat. It was widely acknowledged to be the most refreshing thing that one could drink on a hot day.

"Badiane," I called to the back, *"Sa sow niekh-ne dé!* [Your sow is delicious]!" and I handed a gourdful to Latendeo.

"Det," he refused, *"Nan-il, yo, nan-il way* [Drink up, you, drink it up]."

He watched with a host's pleasure as I downed it and scooped up some more. *"Nan-il way, nan-il; nu dierkh* [Drink up; may it be all gone]," he urged whenever I hesitated; but I needed little encouragement. I scooped out the last gourdful.

"*Touti rek nga nek Serrer* [Just a little bit more time and you'll be a Serrer]," he said with approval.

"You don't have to be Serrer to like *sow*."

"*Wackh nga dug, wackh nga dug* [you speak the truth]."

The drums, which had stopped for a while, now started again, reminding us once again of the approaching event.

"*Ah, boré u Serrer niekh-ne dé!*" he said beside me.

"But you say it used to be better?"

"Today's match is no good at all."

"Halifa is awfully strong."

"He's strong, but he doesn't know how to fight. These youngsters don't know how to fight. Toubabs don't know how to fight. But the Serrer used to know. Back a few years, back in my father's time, then there were some fights..."

He began to drift into one of his dream-like recollections which I loved to hear but which I could never wholly understand because he frequently drifted out of Wolof into Serer, and because the constellation of names and places was called up from a world which didn't exist anymore. He sat straight on the edge of the bed, eyes closed, rocking slightly, his impish face wearing a look of beatific peace as if he were slipping into a soothing bath. I strained to keep track of the names and the thread of the story, but all I received, as usual, was a rich impression of a mythic tapestry whose details I could not quite discern.

"… and my father rode out to N'Diamane and met Gorgi Yatte's grandfather, and he told him that the toubabs were at M'Bouloktane. They talked and talked and decided to ride there to meet them. They rode to the village of N'Dek and called from their horses for ——— to join them ...; and they rode to Talegne and called for ———— to join them ...; until soon the entire region was riding to face the toubabs. And they rode there, and they met them, and the chief of the toubabs told them to put down their arms...; but my father refused, and he cursed them, and he rode back into the countryside with his men..."

"*Konk, konk,*" we heard at the door, and Guedj entered the neg. "*Gorgui Fall, djam ngam* [Mr. Fall, I hope you have peace]?"

"*Gorgui Sene, djam a-rek* [Mr. Sene, I have peace only]."

"*Suma baye da nellow* [My father is sleeping]," he said looking at Latendeo sitting on the edge of the bed with his eyes still closed.

"Gorgui Fall: This afternoon I'm going to eat your money. Boy Serrer is going to win."

"*Mook* [never]! Halifa is his master."

"Today's boré isn't worth a thing," said Latendeo abruptly.

"Listen to my father," Guedj laughed affectionately, "As his body gets weaker his boasting grows stronger."

Latendeo sputtered an indignant protest and fell silent.

"Ma né, Gorgui Fall," said Guedj after a moment, "I've been hearing that if you go back to your country they're going to put you in the army."

"It's the truth."

"It seems to me that you don't want anything to do with war."

"You're right. I don't want anything to do with war."

"Ma né, listen to me a little: If it comes about that you have to go home, and that they want to put you in the army, may you come to my home. I'll give you something to prevent it. Do you hear me?"

"I hear you all right."

"Good. But Gorgui Fall."

"I'm right here."

"War is good."

"War is no good at all."

"War may be no good at all, but I like it."

Guedj had shown me his box of souvenirs from the Algerian war—snapshots of a younger Guedj in uniform standing at attention, firing a rifle behind some sand bags, and so forth. He had described to me something of their life in Algeria, of getting wounded twice, of seeing Paris. As nearly as I could understand it the war had been an adventure. He had learned to read and write and speak French, he had seen the world, he had tasted combat. He had had no consciousness that he was fighting fellow Africans, or that the French were perhaps his real enemy. He had had many friends among the French soldiers. The war was a circumstance that he had been swept up in, and it had been good to him.

Near the end of the war the Frenchman in charge of the mess hall for the Senegalese soldiers had tried repeatedly to force those who were Moslems to eat pork; and Guedj and some others had finally jumped him and killed him. Guedj had returned to Senegal in chains and had been held prisoner in Thies for another year before his brother, young Gana, who had since become chief, had been able to pull enough strings to have him set free.

He expressed no bitterness about this. The whole experience seemed to have been a great opportunity, leaving him more worldly, with the skill of literacy, the memory of places he had seen, of comrades-in-arms, and the fascination with battle.

"War is a good thing," he reiterated now.

"Wackh nga dug," affirmed his father.

I knew that when the students at the university in Dakar had gone on strike a few years before and the president of country, a Serrer, had sent out a call for aid from the countryside—'When Leopold called us,' as Latendeo put it—Guedj had been one of the men from the village who had jumped onto a government truck with gops and machetes and been taken to Dakar prepared to quell the insurrection. The fascination for battle ran in his blood, yet he understood perfectly well that I wanted to limit my taste for it to vicarious participation at the wrestling match.

"Gorgui Fall," he said now as the drums began to swell in the background, "Listen to the griots. I've got to go into town. Until later—today's boré is going to be good."

"Today's boré is no good at all," said Latendeo.

"Listen to my father," Guedj laughed, "You're an old man now. Go challenge Halifa if you want to find out who can wrestle and who can't."

"In the whole countryside, I was the fastest…"

"You're not so fast now that you have three legs instead of two. Gorgui Fall: I'm going now. Until later." We shook hands.

"Sene."

"Fall."

"Sene."

"Fall." And he was out the door, leaving his father and me in an eddy of silence.

"Ah Fall, " said Latendeo, his voice rising with a quaver, "My body hurts me; my eyes can't see anymore; my legs are no longer fast. But dugadugadug, the Serrer used to be strong; and this country used to be a wonderful place."

"I believe you."

"Ma né. Leopold—does he hold discussions with your leader?"

"Sure."

"He has strength; but the country is no good at all anymore."

"Your country is pleasing to me…"

"It was pleasing once—it had no equal—but it's no good at all now."

"You're just old—that's all."

We fell silent.

"Sene," I finally said, "I've got to go get into some good clothes. The boré's about to begin. Will I see you there?"

"You'll see me there, and I'll be dancing and wrestling."

"Good. Until then." We shook hands.

"Fall"

"Sene"

"Fall"

"Sene," and I took my leave.

The drums had increased, and I saw as I crossed over to our house that a crowd had already gathered around the entrance to the arena. I knew that it would be a while before even the preliminary activities actually took place, but since this was the last boré of the season I wanted to be present for the entire event.

Nini was at home with Bity and Baddu; and after we had relaxed for a while and put on fresh clothes, we all went over to the arena.

Outside the entrance confusion reigned as most everyone in the village clamored to get in for free. The drums inside incited the crowd, and it was almost unendurable to hear them so close and yet be separated from them by the visual screen of the fence. Admission was 50 francs CFA—25 for children—but most everyone managed to get in eventually, one way or another. We passed in for free as charter members of the boré committee, and we entered the arena.

The bright expanse of sand in the center was empty as of yet. Surrounding it was a thickening ring of people, clothed in material of all colors and patterns, with the drummers at one side and a shade roof for dignitaries at another. The whole scene was enclosed by a fence about six feet high. It had been made of *basi*, the strongest of the strains of millet, and had stood up well, sagging only at one end where some peeping toms had pressed in too hard upon it the week before. We made our way over to the shade roof, greeting friends as we went, and sat down to enjoy the show.

The arena was filling up with people now, and the younger griots were beginning to relinquish their drums to their elders. It was a gala event. I saw Fatou N'Diaye across the way looking proud and formal in a voluminous multi-layered costume, keeping a flock of her brother Yibou's dressed-up children in front of her like a mother hen. Numerous other Wolof matrons were approaching the occasion with a similar attitude, as if it called for a degree of dignity and decorum which lesser events did not require; but the children chafed under their restraint, and periodically one would embarrass its mother by breaking free of her presence and racing across the empty arena to join some friends on the other side.

Young Gana sat near us in his finest grand bou-bou. With him was a young fonctionaire from N'Goye, dressed in a spotless white robe, who had become a regular spectator the last few weeks; and at his feet sat Ami Laye, who had been desperately flirting with him each time he appeared. Various members of the boré committee and their peers, all of whom would insist on some say in deciding who should wrestle the preliminary bout, were hovering about in the initial stages of argument: Abdou Dieye, Moussa Dieye, Gibril Gadjiaga, Guedj, and several others. Saliou Diouf, who presided over the whole affair, was walking along the inside of the fence behind us throwing sand against it to repel the unseen children who were threatening to collapse it from the other side.

Several wrestlers had arrived and were crouching near the drummers waiting until the time was ripe to begin the pomp and ceremony. I saw Tchiendou N'Diaye standing behind his wives flashing a gold-toothed smile; his lovely light-skinned wife, Awa Fall; and Seidu, proud and aloof; and old Gana, ponderous and senatorial; and countless others. It was to be a momentous event. The appointed wielder of the whip had already made a couple of routine passes around the perimeter of the open space, frightening back the children who formed the inner edge of the crush of spectators.

The drums stopped for a moment, as several wrestlers conferred with M'Baye Diouf the griot, who was manning the biggest drum. Then suddenly, to great tumult, the wrestlers burst into the center and began their counterclockwise dance and strut. With colorful swatches of material tucked into their belts and countless magic charms strapped onto their arms and legs and chest, they paraded flamboyantly around the arena, only occasionally breaking stride to show off, aware that they constituted the merest preliminary to the afternoon's program.

These were all young men from the surrounding countryside who were exercising their adventurous spirits, easing into the showplace of the arena and hoping perhaps to be chosen to wrestle a pick-up match. Mostly they were here to show off and prance around, as they knew that the bigger and more popular wrestlers would join the parade over the course of the next hour or so and out-shine them. They were testing the waters. Next year some of them would be back and try more seriously for a match, letting the new crop of neophytes be the first ones into the arena.

At the first boré of the year the field had been composed almost entirely of these lightweights, the eventual stars of the season not deigning to show themselves that early in the season. We had arrived early that afternoon, expecting to see a series of matches, and had witnessed instead a full three hours of parading, flexing, challenging, and dancing until finally, with dusk falling fast, a match between the two most eager wrestlers had been set up, started, and fought to a finish within the space of a minute. Bity had turned to us with a smile and said *"Djierk-ne* [That's it]," knowing that we would not believe it; and we had left to go to supper.

Since then the matches had improved in quality, and the parade of wrestlers—which seemed, after all, to be the most important part of the whole affair—had grown more interesting as we began to recognize particular fighters and as men with established reputations had begun to participate.

The format since the first afternoon had consisted of one *djoni-djoni* and one *grand combat*, the first being a match arranged on the spot on the basis of crowd reaction to various possible pairings, and the latter being a similar match-up of greater magnitude negotiated by members of the wrestling committee the previous week. The wrestlers in the *grand combat* received an amount of cash, which mounted gradually as the season approached its climax.

The matches, decided by the first fall, with punches allowed, were generally consummated quite quickly and were of unreliable excitement in and of themselves. The fundamental portion of the event, it eventually became apparent, was the long build-up of excitement and tension for which the actual wrestling provided a climax and release.

Normally little happened during the first hour or so as a foundation of arousal was being laid. The wrestlers simply paraded around the circle to the drums, bantering among themselves and showing off to the crowd. Then, gradually, individuals would begin asserting themselves: One would break into the center with a series of acrobatic moves, drawing a response from the spectators and then returning to the periphery; another would confer with the drummers and then dance slowly from the center towards the big drum in a flamboyant display of rhythmic power; or two men would break from the flow to flex at one another and engage in mock combat.

The central gesture of these preliminaries was the challenge, when one wrestler would seize the biggest drum from whoever was playing it, carry it into the middle of the arena, hurl it down in the sand and stand beside it defiantly. Depending on his presence and timing this action may or may not evoke a response from the crowd and from the other wrestlers. Sometimes it was simply ignored in the general clamor; and sometimes it was apparent that the man had not really wanted the challenge to be taken up by anyone. More often, though, another wrestler would accept the challenge by kicking sand on the drum or kicking it over, and the two would square off in dramatic poses. Again, this sometimes failed to be timely or interesting enough to gain any reaction from the people.

As the challenges grew more impressive, however, and as the general level of excitement rose, the exchange of gestures would gain the attention of the crowd; and as this began to occur, the members of the wrestling committee would be thrown into violent debate over the possibilities of such and such a match-up. And thus it would build, with the drummers and wrestlers performing tirelessly until one challenge could excite the crowd to such a level of noise and insistence that the committee members could no longer postpone the match with their arguments. There would be a final rush of debate; Saliou and a couple of others would move to the center and offer the match to the spectators, who would acclaim it; and the match would begin posthaste.

In what seemed a perfect example of Wolof organizational philosophy the committee had appointed Maury Dia as referee, one of the meekest and most ineffectual men in the village. It was against the spirit of the boré to have the wrestlers too severely constrained. Maury would blow his whistle to absolutely no avail when the activity in the middle was intense; but at times of lesser excitement he would be able to provide the element of formal order necessary to keep the affair moving.

In the second wrestling match of the season the *grand combat* had been rather minor affair; but after that the real heavyweights had begun to participate. Halifa arrived at the third match and thereafter became a regular participant with his partner, a smaller man with a talent for provoking the crowd's anger. The latter immediately wrestled and won a *djoni-djoni* the third week and was so controversial that he was picked for a later *grand combat;* but in the grand scheme of things he served only as a hustler and front man for Halifa, who did not deign to indulge in antics himself but merely let his presence and reputation slowly impress themselves upon the populace. Apparently the two men made a regular circuit of matches throughout the region.

Halifa himself was a burly, powerful man whose only departure from a slow rhythmic jog about the arena with the others was to stop occasionally to flex his bicep to a particular portion of the crowd or to show his contempt for a smaller wrestler who had made a challenge by kicking over the drum and glaring at the man. While his partner hustled his way to minor glory and provoked universal outrage by winning his *grand combat*, Halifa emerged as the real potential champion.

His first competition to emerge was Boy Serrer *numero un*, who was smaller but very stocky and was something of a local favorite. He would demonstrate the power of his legs by performing prodigious two-legged leaps about the arena; and he would make a challenge by grasping the great drum by one of its pegs with his teeth and staggering into the center with it. The confrontation between him and Halifa over the challenge drum was awesome, and a *grand combat* was arranged to tremendous popular acclaim. The following week, Halifa disposed of him within 15 seconds.

Meanwhile other prospects showed themselves, chief of whom were Boy Serrer II, Yibou Gaye — a muscular and acrobatic stranger of uncertain provenance — and a couple of winners of the earliest *grand combats* who felt they were ready for the big time. One week a fat and magnificently costumed man named Babacar came all the way from Dakar, accompanied by his own *griot,* who followed him about the ring with his drum. He danced provocatively and effeminately, calling out to young Gana and the other dignitaries to match him against someone and upstaging the other wrestlers. During the following week rumors spread through the village that Babacar was a famous champion, or that he was a *gor-djigen* [homosexual], or both, or that he really couldn't wrestle at all; but the controversy faded when he never showed up again.

Boy Serrer II felled his first opponent with impressive ease. Yibou Gaye — extremely tall, highly reputed, and a magnificent dancer — prevailed over Halifa's partner in an exciting battle, using his greater leverage after sustaining a blow to the face as the two had clinched. And Halifa stalked down and overpowered the acrobat, who was never seen again. Then boy Serrer II took on Yibou Gaye in an epic test of power versus leverage, with fists thrown in for extras. He finally was able to lift the taller man clear of the ground and throw him after ten or fifteen tense minutes of scuffles, punches, and near falls. It was by far the finest match to date.

And so today, finally, the two giants were facing each other; and I shared the simmering excitement running through the crowd. Both were powerful men of obvious talent, ferocity, and magnetism. My preference for Halifa was based on an impression of mental superiority — my sense that he had demonstrated an advantage in class in dealing with a particular irritant with which they had both had to cope.

N'Gor Diop was a young man in the village who was considered half-crazy: He acted crazy enough to receive the exemption of crazy people from the responsibilities and conventions of ordinary life, and sane enough to thoroughly enjoy the benefits of such exemption. Very small, with a slight forward lean and prominent buttocks, and possessed of great energy, he would exploit his ambiguous status with tremendous agility, often to others' embarrassment and frustration. At réunions, for instance, he would often rush up to the dignitaries and greet them half-earnestly and half-mockingly, in such a way that they had to endure the partial embarrassment in order to maintain face; for if they tried to rebuff him he would shift instantly to a full-fledged ingenuousness which made them look cruel or foolish.

It so happened that N'Gor was a fantastic dancer; and once or twice he appeared at the arena dressed in boré costume and paraded with the wrestlers with tremendous enthusiasm, playing to the crowd as he simultaneously parodied and embodied to the hilt the role of a wrestler. This was of general embarrassment to the other wrestlers. Once Maury Dia had tried to eject him from the arena, with such utter failure that he never attempted it again. Clearly N'Gor was a gadfly to be endured. Those who tried to swat him inevitably suffered the embarrassment of missing their mark.

One week towards the end of the season Halifa, Boy Serrer II, and N'Gor were all in attendance. At a point during the build-up of excitement Boy Serer decided to perform a dramatic dance towards the drums, and he consulted with M'Baye Diouf, who moved to the front of the griots with the biggest drum. Boy Serrer then went to the middle of the arena and, as M'Baye Diouf commenced his rhythm, began a slow, powerful march towards the griot. Instantly, there was N'Gor—little, fat-assed N'Gor—dancing up a storm beside him, throwing himself into the dance and making him look clumsy by comparison. Boy Serrer glared at him, but N'Gor only increased his tempo and stared at him with wide-eye good will, gesturing him to keep going, to join him in the dance as his little body bounced wildly to the drums. Boy Serrer finally broke his stride, snapping the tension between himself and the big drum, and sulked away to join the circular flow of the other wrestlers. N'Gor quit his dance with a shrug as if he couldn't do it without Boy Serrer; and he too joined the general flow, now and then cheering to the crowd and urging them to increase their support for him and his fellows.

A little later Halifa grabbed the big drum and hurled it down in challenge in the center. Immediately, before he even had time to spread his palms in invitation to potential opponents, N'Gor darted in from the perimeter, kicked the drum over, and squared off ferociously, flexing his muscles and urging Halifa to close with him. The match was preposterous, but the little man had a manic genius for mockery, and Halifa was clearly challenged. He maintained his composure, however, and looked down at N'Gor with amused disdain, as if he could squash him like a bug were it not beneath his dignity and were N'Gor not perhaps worth saving as a curiosity. This time it was N'Gor who broke off his gesture and returned to the perimeter. Halifa's aura remained undiminished, and the crowd roared.

It was on the basis of this comparison that I favored Halifa; but it promised to be a battle. The arena was abuzz with spectators; and a group of five wrestlers from M'Bomboye had just burst en masse into the ring. One of them had won a *djoni-djoni* early in the season and had since provoked quite a bit of reaction from the crowd because of his obvious conceit. He had a way of puffing out his cheeks as he danced towards the drums which triggered general outrage; but he was not one of the larger wrestlers and had only been awarded that one *djoni-djoni*.

A couple of fonctionaires from Bambey had arrived, and I noticed a number of people from M'Bomboye and beyond who had not made it to previous matches. A contingent from N'Diamane was also in attendance; and N'Djamé Sene, and Yilliman N'Gom, and many more. I saw Latendeo headed our way, pausing to challenge Waly Sene with his cane and then continuing on to greet the fonctionaires to our left. When he greeted us I succeeded in making him take my seat; and while he berated Nina for not visiting him I listened to a breathless story from Baddu, who had just appeared beside me.

He pointed out three men across the ring who he said were Peuhls from the temporary encampment of Peuhl herders outside of N'Dangalma. He had seen them there earlier today, he said, and they had made remarks about him among themselves, not knowing that he was laobé and could understand their language. He had rebuffed them with a masterful torrent of curses in laobé, and now he was frightened because he knew they were carrying knives as all Peuhls were known to do. I assured him that they were just there to attend the boré, and we watched as several higher-caliber wrestlers joined the parade and the drums ratcheted up their tempo once again.

Saliou Diouf was now kneeling and talking with Maury Dia in front of us. Guedj was consulting furiously with Abdou and Moussa Dieye on our right, with Papa Sall trying to wedge himself into the discussion. On our left the beaten Boy Serrer I was kneeling and pointing out one of the wrestlers to young Gana. A roar arose suddenly and ran through the crowd as a group of three wrestlers, including Boy Serrer II, entered the ring with a flourish.

This was it, then. Virtually everyone who would arrive had arrived, with the exception of the great Halifa himself. Challenges began to be made. The boy from M'Bomboye puffed up his cheeks and strutted around and yelled something at Cadere Dia, N'Djamé Sene's *apprenti*, who had been insulting him from the sidelines; but it was evident that no *djoni-djoni* would yet be chosen. Boy Serrer II continued his slow pace around the ring, his companions on either side of him.

Another roar erupted from the entrance, and Halifa's partner ran screaming into the ring, followed more calmly by the great man himself; and they began their customary jog. Once or twice Halifa stopped to flex threateningly at Boy Serer; and the latter responded by staring back and pulling down at the skin below his eyes with two fingers, as if to say, "I see it, and it's not affecting me." The boré was in full swing.

More serious challenges began to be raised, now, and a couple of pairings elicited roars from the crowd. The committee members obviously felt that these were premature, however, and only argued lightly among themselves.

The parade continued. Halifa and his partner stopped at one end, drew some figures in the sand, poked some rolled-up pieces of paper into the sand, set them ablaze, and danced around them, finally stamping them out. The crowd responded loudly; and Boy Serer gave his 'I see it' sign. The excitement mounted. Boy Serer performed the ever-impressive stunt of carrying the drum in his teeth, and several others made very dramatic challenges. Cadere Dia moved as if to challenge the boy from M'Bomboye from the sidelines but was restrained by those around him. The crowd responded with clamors of both approval and disapproval. Some wanted to see Cadere take him on; others were worried that he would get hurt. Saliou and his fellows clearly felt a fiduciary responsibility for Cadere's health and yelled for him to calm down.

The afternoon was beginning to wane, and some sense of urgency was beginning to creep into the responses to possible *djoni-djoni* pairings. Two more challenges met with wide acclaim, but the committee wasn't quite ready to approve a match. Gibril Gadjiaga, Papa Sall, and Guedj were now gesticulating wildly among themselves, their voices lost in the noise of the crowd.

The boy from M'Bomboye now became the center of attention with a cheek-puffing strut and then threw down the challenge drum to a strident din of cheers and jeers. Cadere could no longer restrain himself and broke free of his companions, tearing off his cap and shirt and taking up the challenge in the center of the ring. The two glared at each other with irrepressible dislike. The cries of those calling for Cadere to sit down were lost in the general tumult. Saliou, Abdou Dieye, and Guedj approached the pair slowly, arguing with those behind them and obviously torn between making Cadere sit down and approving the match. As they approached the pair the noise grew louder until they simply could no longer deny the match. They huddled briefly as the opponents remained stock-still and glaring at each other, then talked with each wrestler and sent them apart to their respective companions.

The ring was cleared, and Maury Dia went to the center with his whistle. Cadere rolled up his pant-legs, while across the ring his opponent's handlers un-strapped an elaborate gri-gri from his chest. Maury whistled once for them to appear at the center; and before he could whistle again they were at each other.

Cadere was slightly smaller than his opponent but very strong. After they had grappled once and broken apart the boy from M'Bomboye seemed worried. Cadere advanced ferociously, refusing to rest. His opponent backpedaled, fending him off with his fists; but Cadere pursued relentlessly, got in close, grabbed a leg, and after a few seconds of frozen tension, took him down.

Chaos reigned. Cadere was mobbed by supporters and lifted onto their shoulders. The drummers pounded away furiously. The boy from M'Bomboye was lost from sight. Our portion of the arena was consumed with jubilant pride in Cadere. Gana was out of his seat congratulating Saliou; and Guedj was yelling "I told you he could do it" into Abdou Dieye's ear.

This was an unanticipated delight to the hometown crowd, and celebration continued for a full five minutes while Maury Dia blew his whistle to try to clear the ring. Finally, excitement waned as it became generally acknowledged that it was time to continue. Dusk was falling and there were bigger things to come.

The ring was cleared once more, and the drums fell silent. Boy Serrer and his seconds consulted at one end, making enigmatic gestures among themselves and stripping him of extraneous pieces of material and magic charms. In just his wrestler's loincloth he looked massive. Maury Dia and Saliou stood in the middle; but Halifa was nowhere to be seen. Boy Serer finished preparing himself and stood alone. Still no Halifa.

Boy Serrer had finally retired to hushed consultation with his handlers when suddenly Halifa and his partner ran into the ring spraying liquid from their mouths and jolting the crowd from its silence. The partner held a bottle of the liquid, with which he doused Halifa; and then they both took mouthfuls and sprayed them out again onto the sand of the arena. Boy Serrer gave them his "I see it" gesture from across the way.

Halifa and his partner huddled on the perimeter and lit another fire, then danced it out and engaged in a final consultation. Finally he was ready, and the two men faced each other alone, with only Maury Dia standing between them in the gathering darkness.

The crowd was silent. The two approached each other slowly, easing into their wrestler's crouches. They closed further, eyes locked on one another; and when they came to within five feet of each other, Maury blew his whistle and got out of the way.

The crowd broke its silence as the two men closed and then repelled each other with fierce swings of their fists. They seemed dead even and wary. They traversed the ring several times crouching face to face, feinting and swinging, until finally they grappled together over on the far side.

Colliding in the gloom, they stopped each other cold, both straining for traction in the sand and heaving to lift the other. Neither could gain any advantage, however, and they fell into the crowd together amidst great confusion.

Immediately they were up again and resumed battle near the center. Both landed heavy body blows; and then they clutched each other close in, turning round and round as a pair, with neither able to find the opening, or false step, or leverage to overturn the bulk of the other.

It was becoming difficult to see, and the crowd was frantic. The wrestlers broke again amid a flurry of blows, jockeyed for position, closed again, strained and heaved, broke again; and finally it was too late — they were virtually invisible, even at close quarters. As they separated once again in the darkness, gasping with fatigue and with the crowd screaming in confusion on all sides, Saliou and the others rushed between them calling an end to the whole affair.

I couldn't believe it. We stood for a few moments in the pitch-blackness and then joined the blind crush of bodies moving towards the door. Utter outrage prevailed; the din was deafening. I recognized Seidu pressed against me, and we yelled into each other's ears.

"*Djam dou am chi dukabi goudi gi* [There won't be any peace in the village tonight]," he shouted.

We laughed helplessly at our predicament. I held Nini's hand in the darkness, and we inched with the tight pack of bodies towards the exit, finally finding ourselves expelled, with great relief, into the open night air beyond. We headed up to Séssene, and entering old Gana's compound found Tchab, Sey Dieng, and Sey Tchiao all cooking the evening's *tcheré*.

"*Ma né,*" said Tchab as we greeted each other and sat down, "*Mba boré-gi niekh-ne,*" [I hope the boré was pleasing].

"*Boré-gi!*" said Bity entering behind us, "*Boré-gi niekh-ul dara dara dara* [this boré was not pleasing in any way]!"

Old Gana and Modou N'Gom arrived on his heels.

"*Mba djam le,*" pursued Tchab.

"*Djam am-a-tul fen leygi* [There's no peace anywhere now]," Bity answered.

As if in support of his remark, Gib and M'Baye Tchiao entered at the far side of the compound by Adjuma's hovel, embroiled in argument.

"Mba djam ngen am," Bity called in greeting. They answered in form, but with disgust.

Gana chuckled and began telling me exactly how the *gouni-yi* [the youngsters] had mismanaged the affair. Gib Tchiao came over and agreed, then gave his own theory of how it should have been handled.

As Tchab put the tcheré bowl down among us and ladled out the sauce, an angry burst of Serrer arose in the next compound. Bity listened, then laughed and said that it was Tchiachi berating his wife for not having his tcheré ready. Another voice joined in which I recognized as that of Tchiachi's wife's brother, apparently arguing with Tchiachi.

"*Boré-gi, ki kai mome amult gen njerine* [This boré was completely useless]," said Gana as if disposing of the matter from his mind; and he disappeared into his neg where he began making preparations for a trip to Dakar the next day. We could hear the slight rasping sound as he grated kola nuts into his little tin container.

"*Lekilen,*" Bity insisted, and we turned to the meal. We laughed as we heard Latendeo's angry voice approach beyond the fence and then fade out as he entered his own compound. We ate until we were stuffed. Baddu entered, ate a little, and described his disgust with the whole affair so eloquently and at such length that we finally had to tell him to be quiet.

M'Baye Tchiao came over to join us and we all finally relaxed on the sand with cigarettes in the cooling night air. A comical, deaf old Serrer man came in to buy tobacco from Gana, who emerged and unrolled the cloth in which he kept it wrapped. The two examined each leaf closely, commenting on its merits and proposed price, and we all laughed among ourselves at the facial expressions of the man who, being deaf, could not hear us.

Suddenly an uproar arose from Latendeo's compound. Women screamed, and male voices let loose angry torrents of Serrer. Bity, M'Baye, and Gib all listened for a few seconds and then ran outside towards the commotion. I followed as the clamor continued and emerged into the open space between the two compounds to see Guedj, lit by flashlights, waving a pistol over his head and being restrained by four or five men. They finally succeeded in calming him and ushering him back to his compound, and I returned to where we had eaten.

Bity returned moments later, explaining that Guedj and young Gana had had a big argument and that Guedj was threatening to kill his brother. He said that he was going down now to the main part of the village to find Gana and try to prevent any escalation.

As he left, Gib and M'Baye reentered, commenting disgustedly to each other; and then as a commotion arose once again beyond the fence they ran back out towards the other compound. We heard their voices join others in argument while Tchab beside us clucked her disapproval and launched into her familiar recitation of the virtues of a sober, peaceful, hard-working life.

The commotion finally subsided, but Gib and M'Baye Tchiao did not return. We sat and made small talk with Tchab for a while, but our minds were elsewhere as well. The evening calm of the compound and the cook fires had been torn apart—and it would not return tonight. Tonight there was a spirit loose in the village whose disquieting touch reached everywhere. The very ordinary activities of the women sitting in the sand at the heart of the compound took on a tense and threatened air. Finally we rose and took our leave, bidding goodnight to Tchab and Sey Dieng and Sey Tchiao, and drawing a nod from the silent Adjuma.

"*Fananilen ak djam* [May you pass the night in peace]."

"*Amin* [Amen]."

"*Yalla nenyu yeo ak djam* [May Allah let us wake in peace]."

"*Amin.*"

Later, as we lay back in the hammocks and let the night air wash over us, we could hear continued quarrels erupting over in Séssene, punctuated by snatches of commotion making their way up from the *dukaba*. Seidu had been right: There would be no peace in the village tonight. It was a long time before we felt calm and weary enough to crawl in under the mosquito netting and try to sleep.

Chapter 7

Coq

Coq

The day had cooled. The sun was falling low behind the *bentenyi* trees as I walked slowly through the sand at their feet where the governor's réunion had taken place six months before. The dried sweat on my neck and brow served to emphasize the precious relief of this hour of the day — *ker gi sedé:* when the shadows are cool.

The cook fires had started. A layer of soft blue smoke hung low over the Serrer compounds on either side of me, against the dark green presence of the trees behind. Luminous in the late afternoon light, it was beginning to waft ever so gently out across the bordering fields of grass, outdistanced by random voices of children and the occasional lazy protest of a cow. A long, hot day was finally coming home to the cool sand of the compounds and the warmth of the fires.

I was tired, but the subversive yielding of the sand to my steps was soothing now that the demands of the day had passed. I took my time. Up ahead of me, I could see more blue smoke drifting lazily in my direction from the Séssene compounds across the village.

In the *dukaba* a few men were out strolling before going in for the evening meal. Amadou Badiane, normally loquacious, merely nodded as he passed doing his prayer beads. Nopili, the main well, was deserted of women, with only their footprints in the mud around it giving evidence of the day's activity. And as I finally headed my way up the expanse of sand towards the house, the cry of "Allaaaah Akbaaaaar…," arose from the dukaba behind me. Now it was *takusan*—the time for evening prayers. *Ker gi sedé* had faded to *takusan*.

This was a time to be savored—a time when the heat of the day and the labors of the day were past, and life came down to the women on the sand of the compounds cooking the evening meal. *Tcheré*, it would be tonight—*tcheré* it was every night—a sand-textured mash of steamed millet enhanced by sauce. We had come to love it. After the planting and the cultivating and the harvesting; after the stalks had all gone to fences and negs, and the tops had been chopped up in the granaries; and after the grain had been separated in the wind and pounded and sifted and pounded again; after all of this it came down to the cooking on the sand of the compound over a fire of sticks gathered *chi-alabi*. *Tcheré*—country fare—to be eaten with a sauce of peanuts, salt, water, and whatever leaves, berries or nuts were ripe in the countryside. It all came down to this.

Each family had its *rabbs*, or spirits, which lived down in the ground among the roots of the trees. In every compound, near the base of a tree, there would be a little cluster of old millet-pounding pestles buried up to all but a foot of their length in the earth and stained with offerings of milk. These homely little shrines seemed to form the spiritual center of a family's existence, with the outer fence of the compound defining the boundary between the family enclave and the unpredictable world beyond.

And it was on the ground beside these tap-lines to the spirits that the women spent their lives. They went to the well, they went chi-alabi to gather sticks for firewood and ingredients for their sauce, they worked their fields; but essentially they lived their lives at the heart of the compound at the source of family power. The clearest image I have of Tchab Dieng or Sey Tchiao or Sey Dieng or almost any of the women we knew is of them sitting flat on the ground, legs unbent in front of them, sifting millet, hulling peanuts or performing some such other daily task. And one of the strongest qualities they seemed to embody was that of inertia: They were not going anywhere. *Tog rek mo backh*, was the phrase that Tchab uttered with reliable frequency: Just sitting home is good.

The women kept a society of their own which was largely separate from that of the men; and it seemed that the incredible basic-ness of their lives gave them a centeredness which made much of the frantic world of their men essentially irrelevant to them. The men were more active and political; but the women stayed right there on the ground at the heart of the compound. And sooner or later it all come down to them.

Their world was largely inaccessible to me, and I was largely irrelevant to them. They seldom asked questions about our own country as the men did. Out in the countryside, beyond the scope of our close acquaintances, they sometimes looked at me in abject disbelief when I spoke to them, as if the very idea of a toubab speaking Wolof were an impossibility.

Dusk was falling as we walked over to dinner. Adjuma was reclining beside his hovel and nodded to our greetings as we passed into the compound. M'Baye Tchiao was using the fading light to put the finishing touches on a chick house for his mother Tchungass, with his brother Gib close at hand giving advice. We greeted them, and Sey Dieng and Sey Tchiao called to us to come eat. I squatted and took a few handfuls of Sey Tchiao's tcheré while Nini continued to the other side of the compound. Modou Tchiao, a healthy little boy of about three, accompanied me at the bowl.

"M'Baye Tchiao," I said, *"neg u Adjuma raffet-ne leygi!"*

He looked up from his work and gestured with his head towards Adjuma in hopeless disgust: "He won't even go in it. He says it needs to be moved about a foot in that direction."

"He'll go in when it rains, " I said.

He shrugged with a smile. "Who knows; he's worse than a horse, that one." M'Baye Tchiao also had charge of Gana's horse, which was out of sight behind a fence behind his brother's neg, and it was a matter of some debate which constituted more of a chore.

Sey Dieng took Adjuma a bowl of tcheré.

"*Aitcha, aitcha, aitcha, aitcha,*" he called suddenly over to me. "*Aitcha nyu rare; aitcha nyu rare* [Come on, let's eat]!"

"*Backh-ne. Sur na,*" I declined politely. "*Merci. Sur na way.*"

M'Baye Tchiao was making the chick house of flattened-out tin cans nailed to a frame of sticks lashed together with vine. Tchungass was very pleased, as something had been killing her hen's chicks in the night. We had put some of our own hens' eggs under her hen, and three of them had hatched; but only one was left, which she now rounded up to show me.

"*Ma né,*" said Sey Tchiao, "*Dingendi fetch té* [Are you two going to dance tonight]?"

"*Wow, wow,*" I assured her. There was going to be a big *coq* [dance] tonight here in Séssene. "*Mba dinga fetch yo it* [I hope you're going to dance too]."

She said she would.

Gib Tchiao was saying that he had unloaded cans like these at the dock in Dakar where he had spent the previous dry season prior to work in the fields. They came from France, he said. He began describing his plans to go to Abidjan—plans which I had heard from many mouths. Abidjan was the Promised Land just as surely as Tambacunda was Siberia—more so than France or Amérique. It was every man's dream to go to Abidjan and get rich. Bity was always mentioning that so-and-so had a son in Abidjan, or so-and-so's husband had been there for three years and was reputedly making a fortune. It seemed that the official governmental system whose keys were literacy and bureaucracy was overlaid upon a popular subsystem that was universally accessible. Someone always knew someone who worked on the docks or who had an uncle who did such and such; and sometimes it seemed that the entire social fabric was woven of a complex accumulation of favors. Getting to Abidjan was not an impossibility for a villager; it merely required patience—the one substance which everyone possessed in limitless abundance.

Gaye, an ancient crony of Tchab's who lived in the adjoining compound, had often told me that her son was far away to the south, which others interpreted for me as Abidjan; that he was making a lot of money and was coming home soon. I couldn't help but doubt the ability of this ditzy old woman to be in contact with her son in the Ivory Coast, not to mention the likelihood that her son was actually there. One day, however, she proudly announced to me that he had returned; and sure enough, there he was.

Seck, his name was, and he appeared to have brought back with him an unlimited quantity of cash. Nobody knew quite what it was that he had done in Abidjan—Bity thought he had sold sunglasses and wristwatches on the street—but he had announced that he was home *en congé* [on vacation] for three months. By now he had been home twice that long and was driving poor Tchiachi, his nephew and the only other male in the compound, out of his mind. While Tchiachi worked about the compound, Seck would recline in his neg listening to a battery-powered record player; and while Tchiachi was out working in the fields, Seck would be strolling under a parasol with the profligate Kiné N'Gom on one arm and another griot woman on the other. Everyone laughed at his indolence; but his money talked, and it hadn't yet run out.

Gib was now outlining his plan of how to get passage south on a ship. M'Baye Tchiao said he had once attempted the journey by land. He had gotten as far as the Casamance [the southernmost region of Senegal], he said, and was walking *chi-alaba* when he caught sight of group of men with spears and feathers in their hair. He had hidden in the bushes until they were gone and then headed immediately back home. That had been enough for him.

Sey Tchiao said she was going to *"tog rek* [just sit tight]."

Tchungass agreed. *"Tog di wackhtan rek mo backh* [Just sit and talk, that's the good life]," ran her version of the familiar homily.

"Senegal backh-ul," Gib said now in a refrain that I had heard too many times before. "When you go back to America, I'll go with you." Delivered with a smile, the familiar phrase always held an underlying note of seriousness.

I maintained that he wouldn't like it in America, that he would be lonely, that it would be as difficult for him as it had been for us when we had first come to the village—except worse, because people there were less hospitable. He would miss the village, I said. There would be nothing, for instance, that could compare with the coq that we were going to have that night.

Tchungass agreed heartily. Sey and Sey supported her. M'Baye Tchiao, I knew, had the village too much in his blood to ever leave again, however much he was forced to agree with his brother's appraisal of it. But Gib was addicted to the city, and I knew that he would return to Dakar and await his opportunity. All it required was patience.

I rose to go to the far end of the compound, taking my leave and trying to interest Modou in shaking my hand.

"Mangi dem sa keur leygi rek [I'm coming over to your place right now]," Adjuma interjected from his hovel. "I'm going to spend the night there."

"You'll be awfully lonely, then," I responded, "I'm just going over here."

"*Wackhnga dug, kai; wackhnga dug.*"

Over at the opposite end sat Nini, old Gana, Tchab, Bity, his wife N'Djoli, and Modou N'Gom. I greeted them, and Tchab and N'Djoli invited us to eat. Tchab put her bowl down among us, splashed some *ndowal* around the periphery and handed us the tin can of water for washing our hands.

Gana had been showing Nini a coil of stripped baobab bark, which he was soaking overnight to make into rope for the hammock we were going to send to her grandmother.

"Do you see this, Mina," he said with his adamant mispronunciation of her name: "When I've made this into rope, and two more like it, and we add it to the rope I've already made, we'll have enough for the hammock. It's going to be two strands wider than the last, and the reinforcing in the seat will be longer. That griot you got that first hammock from didn't know anything. Your grandmother is going to see something beautiful."

Bity poked me surreptitiously, as we both knew that he himself had done most of the weaving of the last hammock because his father's eyes were failing. Gana would get the money, which he would use for his bane-bane; but Bity had learned the skill himself now, and was planning to weave one of his own.

Tchab's tcheré was delicious, with some leaves in the ndowal we had never tasted before. Each of us would dig away at the millet on our side of the bowl until the sauce was exhausted, and then we would call for more ndowal. There was one round, mushy berry in the sauce tonight which neither of us cared for but which Tchab was careful to distribute to each of us in turn. We would flip them around the inside perimeter of the bowl in the dark—like roulette croupiers—when Bity's and Modou N'Gom's hands were at their mouths.

Coq

Finally we were full and sat back to relax. N'Djoli passed a tin can of water, I produced a guru, and we all talked about the evening's festivities.

The occasion of the *coq* was the controversial arrival of N'Dik Sene's new wife. He had courted her at her home in M'Bour during the early part of the dry season and had exhausted his limited funds in trying to meet her father's demand for a bride price. The father was still not satisfied, but N'Dik felt that he had paid enough and apparently the woman did too. He had enlisted N'Djamé Sene's aid, and today they and Aliou Diouf and N'Gagne Tchiao had disappeared in N'Djamé's truck to steal her away from M'Bour and bring her back to the village. They were expected any time now, and tonight's coq would be the traditional celebration for when a man brought a new wife to live in his own compound.

Opinions varied as to whether N'Dik's abduction was justified or just plain brazen and disrespectful. When Tchab went out of earshot behind her neg, Bity mentioned that she and her cronies were up to something related to the event. The old women of Séssene had a mysterious society, which seemed to be viewed with both amusement—because they were old women—and respect—because they had certain powers. Bity had told me that sometimes they would focus on a particular woman whom they felt had been disrespectful and demand some sort of recompense from her, with which she always complied because they were capable of doing her harm. He said that his father had seen them cause a healthy bull to collapse and die simply by circling it and waving their kerchiefs at it.

One night when we had arrived for dinner Tchab had been busy in her neg engaging in some sort of private preparations. While we ate N'Djoli's tcheré she had emerged with a warm shawl and a carefully wrapped bundle and proceeded to join ten or fifteen of her peers outside the compound; and they had all set off singing into the pitch-dark night.

Bity had said that one of their peers had died in N'Diamane and that they were headed there, but that no one really knew what they were up to. I knew that the path they were taking passed a certain hollowed-out gigis tree, which Seidu had warned me should never be approached at night.

We talked about N'Dik's negotiations with his new wife's family, which had proceeded over the course of several months. Young Gana had consistently helped N'Dik throughout this period. Bity described in detail, for not the first time, exactly how much he had paid for N'Djoli—how many cows, how much cash, how much labor, how much rice, how much palm oil, etcetera. With Bity also, young Gana had been of assistance, as had his *nidiaye* [maternal uncle], who controlled the cattle of his matrilineage.

Bity's marriage had not worked out well. N'Djoli was not a cheerful person and did not enliven the life of the compound. She had periods of depression, during which Tchab would tell her how lazy she was. She had had two still-borne children and one who had died after three days. When we had first come to the village she had been living with her mother in her original village, but Bity had finally lured her back by giving her a new *complète* [coordinated outfit] and the money to have her gums and lips tattooed. She was still an unhappy woman, however. Bity had told us that she was pregnant again, and we all hoped a child would make a difference. He had procured some *garab* to protect her and was considering the possibility that the same malevolent being—*a nit coo bunn*—had been entering her stomach each time, just to tire her out and make mischief. If the next child was still-borne, he was going to cut a secret notch in its ear before burying it so that he would recognize it if it pulled the trick another time. It was never clear to us what he would do then.

In any case, however, Bity still mourned the hefty bride price which he had paid for N'Djoli. He had never had that much wealth either before or since.

Old Gana said that he could remember when the bride price would consist of a piece of steel and a glass bottle, as well as some cows, which would be paid to the head man of the bride's matrilineage. The price nowadays was largely cash, paid more often than not to the father himself. The government was trying to discourage the institution altogether.

I wondered now about N'Dik's new wife and how she would make out in the compound with his first wife and mother.

"It will be fine," said Bity with his eternal optimism.

"She's going to miss her family," said N'Djoli.

"She's going to miss M'Bour," said Gib Tchiao.

N'Dik's compound was rather decrepit and joyless. It seemed to me that it would be hard for her; but maybe she could make the same difference that N'Djémi Faye had made in this compound. N'Djémi had come to Bity, her nidiaye, from her village on the road to M'Bah Faye, to live here and be married out of his compound. She was bright, quick and cheerful and had made the place sparkle with good feeling. She got along well with Tchab, who tended to be rather sober and resigned, playing tricks on her, helping her, and coaxing her into good humor. I remembered especially the little celebration of Tamharit—after the tcheré had been eaten, after the rabbs had been given their offerings of milk, and after we had made secret wishes into a gourd—when she had beaten a rhythm on an overturned baignoir for all the children of the surrounding compounds to dance to.

N'Djémi had married, though, and her husband had taken her to live in Dakar. Tchab did not get along well with N'Djoli, and the compound was not the same. N'Dik's new wife was going to have to go through a long period of feeling out her relationships with the women in her new compound, with the women of Séssene, with the entire village whom she encountered at the well.

Everyone was eager for her arrival, however—if and when it occurred—and the prospect of the coq had generated great excitement. Sobel N'Gom was coming in from N'Diamane to sing, along with his personal chorus, and some griots from N'Dondol Oulof would be doing the drumming. It would be a fine affair.

Old Gana was playing with Modou Tchiao now, poking his great, calloused finger in his face; and Tchab was carding some cotton that she had grown in a little patch chi alabi and which she would have woven into an undergarment by a weaver across the village after she had spun it herself into thread.

Gana disappeared into his neg to get a heavy sort of shawl. At this time during the dry season it became quite cold at night. Gana would keep a fire on the sand of his neg at night consisting of two good-sized loges whose ends were smoldering, which he would push together for flame and heat but which would burn away from each other, creating no hazard. He had made his neg of certain larger-than-normal dimensions so that some extraordinary number of men could sleep in it in the event of an important funeral or *ngenté*. Its sides were woven of a thin, straight reed rather than millet stalk, which made fine, tightly woven panels.

Little Abdou Dieye wandered in from Latendeo's compound to give a message to Tchab from N'Diaye, young Gana's mother; and we had begun talking about Sobel N'Gom when suddenly we heard N'Djamé's truck approach rapidly and stop in the middle of Séssene between our compound and N'Dik's. Modou N'Gom, N'Djoli, and the two Seys all ran out to join a throng that was already surrounding the truck, while the rest of us maintained our composure and waited to meet the new arrival later. Before long we heard the preliminary drumming begin over in N'Dik's compound, its rhythm calling out to all of Séssene in the darkness that the abduction had been a success.

"*Ma né,*" asked Tchab, "*Dingendi fetch?*" We assured her that we would, and that we expected her to do the same.

Baddu entered the compound now, and we asked the same of him. He had never danced at a big dance before but was feeling that it was about time to reveal himself as a red-blooded young man. All during the previous week he had been taking Modou N'Gom behind our house to practice, persuading Modou to beat out a rhythm for him while he danced.

"*Barkiallah, dina fetch* [You're damn right, I'm going to dance]," he told us now, flashing a white toothed smile in the firelight. "*Suma gunyu bay, dina fetch bu backh.*" Nini kidded him about all his practicing while I asked Bity when Sobel would arrive. He smiled and said he had arrived some time ago and would probably begin shortly. Baddu couldn't sit still, and his excitement quickly infected us. We took leave to go and put on sweaters and told the others we would meet them at the dance.

N'Dik's compound was crowded with people, as the griots continued their drumming and Sobel prepared to sing. N'Djamé Sene's Coleman lantern threw light on the surrounding faces and up against the sheltering bentenyi tree. Sobel and his entourage were setting up at the base of the tree. We went over to speak to him. A shy little man in a dusty green boubou, he often stumbled over his words to others' amusement, especially when he spoke Wolof. We chatted over the din of the drums, as he made sure that the two chairs that he needed were positioned correctly, that there was sufficient room behind him for his chorus, and that the heavy wooden mortar that had been provided produced the proper resonance. Over his shoulder he carried a small leather pocketbook, given him by some grateful patron, which held two pomegranate-sized stones from the seashore near M'Bour. These he would use to beat out a rhythm on the mortar as he held it in his lap. He consulted with the lead griot and then excused himself. We chatted with his partner Modiane M'Bao, asking about various friends in N'Diamane who were absent tonight.

We spotted N'Dik across the circle, and he came over to greet us. A radiant host, he ushered us though a crowd to his neg to meet the new arrival. It was quite dark inside, and I only recognized a couple of the seven or eight women seated about the neg. N'Dik's stolen bride was seated on the bed between two other women and lowered her head with embarrassment when we shook hands. She was quite pretty and wore a new green *complète*, plastic sandals and shiny gold earrings. The blue-black tattoo around her mouth stood out around the lighter brown of her face. She was obviously shy about meeting a pair of toubabs. N'Dik ushered me out and into another neg, this one full of men, while Nini remained with the women for a while.

In this neg were gathered N'Dik's father old Bity, his brother Adjuma, Sobel N'Gom and several other men from Séssene and N'Diamane. I greeted them all around and sat down on the edge of a bed. N'Dik produced a guru, which we shared around the room. The scene was rather like a star's dressing room before a performance, with Sobel drinking from a quart of beer provided by his host and responding only distractedly to others' attempts at conversation. He had taken off his bou-bou and was staring trance-like at the wall in front of him, which had been lined with colored ads from old French magazines to keep out the dry season breeze. I talked with Adjuma about his efforts to get a job in Bambey, and with old Bity, who was a little bit drunk and playing the buffoon. I shared some of Sobel's beer and then talked with N'Dik about his escapade. He was extremely pleased with himself and with the occasion, but his pleasure seemed to have an edge of anxiety.

Evidently he was not in the clear yet: His new wife's family might still decide to make trouble.

Finally, Sobel finished his beer, announced that he was ready and left the neg. I followed with the others and went to the edge of the circle where Nini was already sitting with Guedj, Baddu and Bity. The lantern still blazed against the faces and the tree. The night air was chilly, and everyone was anxious to begin.

Sobel had donned his bou-bou again and was consulting with his companions at the base of the tree. Now he was sitting down and hoisting the big mortar onto his lap; and now he was testing its sound with his stones. Thunk, thunk, it sounded—a high, solid, hardwood sound distinct from that of the drums. Thunk, thunk, thunk, The griots stopped their drumming, and the mortar reverberated alone. Thunkety, thunkety, thunkey thunk from Sobel, and then the drummers answered with a jumbled flurry. Thunkety thunkety thunkety thunk said the stones again, and again the drummers answered, this time together. Again Sobel, and again the drummers; again the rocks, and again the drums. Then Sobel continued his rhythm, and the griots joined him to establish a constant tattoo, the rocks against the mortar maintaining something of a treble beat.

They continued this for a while, with Sobel beating out rhythms of remarkable complexity, until he suddenly raised one rock high and yelled out his first, long phrase in Serrer. The crowd responded with shouts of approval and he repeated the same gesture twice with different messages. This was no shy little Sobel now, stumbling over his words. He was strong and authoritative, fully in command of the words he belted out, fully in command of the show. He paused to shed his bou-bou and the lantern flashed against his bare arms and chest as he resumed the performance. From across the circle it seemed as though the repetitive movements of his short arms bore little relationship to the complex beat reverberating from the mortar. He pounded away tirelessly at the base of the tree, and the frenetic *clackety clackety* would break to the slow *clank clank* of his left hand when he raised the right high and let loose another phrase.

Everyone around us was beaming and yelling approval. Guedj poked me and simply nodded his head towards Sobel with a knowing smile. Baddu let loose a torrent of appreciation, and Bity and I tried to push him into the ring. Somebody handed down a guru from behind and we shared it amongst us.

Sobel moved into the body of his song now. He and Modiane would sing a set of short phrases, and the chorus of those behind them would repeat it. He and Modiane would sing, the chorus would answer, and there would be just drumming for a while; and then they would sing again. This continued until Sobel finally took a break, with the drummers continuing. At this point the first, youngest girls burst into the middle to dance. There were the usual cries from people who wanted to dispense with the immaturity and giggling of the younger dancers, but they had no effect. The girls could not be denied. I was impatient for the long buildup to be over with, and I got up to walk around outside the circle while the children danced. The circle of people, jammed tight on the inside, loosened on the outer perimeter. I wandered amongst others of similar mind out where the shadows from the lantern merged with the enveloping night. Beyond the compound fence, all was dark.

Waly Sene—budding entrepreneur that he was—had set up a little stand by the entrance to the compound and was selling cigarettes, gurus, Medina biscuits, hot candies and Hollywood gum. I shared a cigarette with him, bought a package of Medina biscuits and sat down in the cool sand to chat.

"*Bonjour, Monsieur le Toubab,*" I heard from behind me.

"*Bonsoir, Monsieur le Nit Coo Nyul* [Good evening, Mr. Black Man]," I responded.

It was Nyellor — comical, one-eyed Nyellor — who had been a friend of sorts ever since he had taken four times longer than he should have to put up the fence for us and had failed to return my machete until I had to go looking for it a month later. He was possessed of enormous, rather spastic energy, which erupted at odd moments. He greeted me in his customary creative, and acrobatic, manner, using combinations, permutations and variations of the familiar daily greetings.

"*Djam doo lay, barikala; nanga def-a-def-a-def?*" and so forth. Then, "*Monsieur Fall — Dow djunde Valda?*" He produced from his pocket a fistful of about ten little round tins of Zorro mentholated balm, from the Valda Laboratories in Rufisque. I laughed and refused, and he sat down.

"I hope you didn't steal those," I told him.

"*Mook!*"

I ripped open the brown paper package of Medina biscuits and shared them with Waly and Nyellor. Made in Dakar, the tiny dry biscuits were the minimal imaginable bakery product, more or less comparable to oyster crackers. I held one on my tongue until it had sogged through and then crushed it against the roof of my mouth. We had trained ourselves in such simple pleasures.

"Come on," nagged Nyellor, "buy some Valda. It's good for you; it will keep the flies off your sores." He opened one and waved it under my nose. The menthol pierced my nostrils.

"You've got to tell me where you got it."

"I can't do that."

"Then you'll have to try someone else."

"Hey Waly," he tried, "Why don't you buy my Valda?"

Behind us we heard the stacatto of Sobel's stones joining the drums and we rose, leaving Waly at his lonely outpost. I slipped back into place at the front edge of the circle, while Nyellor tried to sell Nini and Guedj some Valda and then moved on.

The dancers were older now, but people were growing impatient: the excitement was not building as it should. After a few more dancers we saw Sobel shake his head in disapproval; and then his right hand went high as he called out with a touch of anger to the crowd. Three more phrases and he wrestled the mortar from his lap, threw his stones down in the sand and danced around the circle with a short, powerful staccato strut—two steps on his knees, two on his feet, two on his knees and so forth, exhorting the crowd as he went. The noise level rose immediately, and as he resumed his seat two mature women burst into the ring to dance. He strutted back in, dancing around the two women, and then sat down and took up his mortar—striking it with renewed energy and drawing another pair of dancers into the center. We were on our way now. The designated whipper sprang into operation to keep the crowd at bay.

Baddu had danced once while I had been gone, and he danced again now, a trifle gawky but earnest, his dark brow furrowed and his eyes flashing as he tried to keep some equilibrium amidst his own flailing limbs. It was a solid performance, and we welcomed him back a hero. Some older men were beginning to dance now. Their general style was much more acrobatic and flamboyant than the women, but as far as I could perceive, it was considerably less complex and skilled. The dominant style consisted of making great leaps in place while windmilling the arms, and hissing loudly through the teeth. When performed well it could be quite exciting, as N'Gagne Tchiao now demonstrated with athletic abandon until the set finally ended and both Sobel and the griots took a break. The din of excited voices carried on where the drums had left off, and the circle collapsed as people took their ease. I could see a crowd around Waly's snack stand now, and across the way Nyellor was trying to peddle his mentholated balm to Saliou Diouf and a crowd of other men. I shared the rest of my Medina biscuits, and we all kidded Baddu about his triumphant dance.

When the dancing resumed emotions were running high. The lamp, which had been faltering, had been replenished, and Sobel built up steam in a hurry. By the time three of the women had danced, excitement had already climbed to its former peak. N'Djoli Dia danced now, with N'Gagne Tchiao coming out behind her before she was even finished. Now Yara Sene danced; now Fat Dia; now Ami Laye.

I had danced once before, at a big funeral, and was trying to get up enough nerve to do it again. It was difficult to choose an opening, however, because an instant of hesitation would allow another dancer to seize the opportunity and jump into the ring. I tensed in anticipation and my heart raced. Twice I allowed the perfect instant to pass me by. Yara was dancing again, and as her flurry began to fade, I lurched forward and suddenly found myself in the middle of the circle staring with disbelief at my own feet in the sand as an enormous roar of approval arose from all around. I leapt into the air and began waving my arms. The din engulfed me, and the scene froze before my eyes with a sensation of absolute silence. I stayed in the air too long on one of my leaps, and I could feel myself losing the rhythm. I began to panic. I had considered doing a front handspring, and I seized upon that now as a way out of my predicament. I took a few quick steps towards the drummers, flung my hands down to meet the ground in front of me and started to summersault as the sand shifted treacherously beneath my palms. My heels hit first, I waved my arms desperately, and I finally gained my balance without sprawling backwards. The crowd went wild, and Sobel threw down his mortar and did a quick, supportive strut about the ring.

The rest of the set passed in a daze. Nini danced, and Guedj danced; and N'Gagne Tchiao again, and Yara. Then the drummers finally took a break, and everyone milled about once again in the cool night air.

When the drums began again for the final set, the older women began to dance, some with babies on their backs. Watching the babies virtually welded to their mothers' bodies, bouncing and spinning to the drums in the night, we marveled at the thought of the memories being laid down in their heads—how strong would be the pull of the drums when they were grown. Some of them even appeared to sleep, their little cheeks pressed against their mothers' backs as they danced furiously beneath them. The lantern began to falter again, making its light flare bright and dim against the gathered faces, the drummers, the overhanging branches of the bentenyi. The old women finally finished off the set, with Tchiab Dieng among them and Moussane Diouf with her chinkling bracelets; and finally it was over. The drums stopped, and people began rising, taking their leave, and disappearing into the surrounding night.

We remained seated, leaning back in the sand and relaxing as the occasion evaporated before us. The crowd thinned quickly. The griots were consulting with some of the older women near the negs. Sobel and his entourage were leaving, but several men remained and were now erecting a pole of about ten feet in height, more or less in the center of the circle where the dance had taken place.

The compound was almost empty when I became aware of a commotion behind us, where it appeared that a few stragglers were being shoved unceremoniously out the exit. At the same time old N'Diaye—young Gana's mother—approached us, and we rose to greet her.

"What are you doing here?" she demanded abruptly, ignoring the courtesy of a greeting. "You shouldn't be here." She stared at us with a look of total lack of recognition. Her face, usually pleasant and dreamy as she sat on a mat in her compound, was adamantly set—intense yet inaccessible.

"Bity," she appealed to him behind us, "Get them out of here. Go on! Get away from here! Get!" She turned away before we could answer, joining Tchab, Gaye and several others of her peers in clearing the compound.

We hurried out. I was a little frightened. I hadn't been able to find any connection when I looked into N'Diaye's eyes and had lost my grasp of what was happening. I asked Bity if we had done anything wrong and he said that the old women were going to have a dance of their own—that he didn't really know what they were up to, but that they had retained the griots and had sworn them to secrecy. I asked again if they had any complaints with us. He said that they hadn't—that they approved of us, thought we were respectful and so forth.

We bade him goodnight at the edge of Séssene and walked out under the stars to our own house across the way. The night air was chilly, and the sand glowed dimly in the starlight.

Inside our fence all was quiet save for the munching of the horses. We lay in the hammocks for a while despite the chill—smoking cigarettes and relaxing, exhausted. The sounds of voices faded out, and then the drums recommenced over in N'Dik's compound. The old women were going about their business. We might find out tomorrow what they had been up to—or we might not. The muffled rhythms rose and fell and gradually took their place in the enveloping darkness. Soon we were just two cigarettes glowing in the dark under an African night crammed full of stars.

Abdou Dieye and the big bentenyi